SUPER INTERESTING STORIES FOR CURIOUS KIDS

Over 100 Fascinating Stories About History,
Science, Inventions, Discoveries And Much
More To Inspire Young Readers

JORDAN MOORE

ISBN: 979-8-88768-027-9

CONTENTS

INTRODUCTION 1

HISTORY... 2

That Time Abraham Lincoln Fought A Duel 3

The Year Of The Four Emperors...5

Franz Ferdinand Escaped One Assassination Attempt...
Only To Fall Into Another!..7

Fidel Castro's Exploding Cigar...9

The Puritans Who Banned Christmas................................10

The Dead Pope Who Was Put On Trial!..............................12

The Destruction Of Pompeii...14

Ra, Ra, Rasputin!..16

Did You Know? 18

SCIENCE 19

The Big Bang Is Still Warming The Universe!......................... 20

Taxicab Numbers: The Story Behind Math's Most Amazing
Digits.. 22

Dmitri Mendeleev And The Organization Of The Elements 25

Why Does Uranus Spin On Its Side?................................... 27

Bananas Are Radioactive! 29

Isaac Newton's Apple 30

Did You Know? 33

INVENTIONS 34

Hedy Lamarr: The Hollywood Star Turned Inventor 35

The Dutch Sailors Who Invented Brandy 37

The Kitchen Mishap That Gave Us Corn Flakes.........................39

Why Did Early Champagne Bottles Keep Exploding? 40

The Tragic Story Of The CPR Dummy 42

The Chef Who Made Up Nachos On The Spur Of The
Moment!..44

Notes About Post-Its 45

How Saccharin Was Invented By Accident 46

Did You Know? 47

DISCOVERIES 48

Darwin's Finches And The Discovery Of Evolution 49

Race To The Bottom: How Scientists Discovered The
Coldest Possible Temperature..51

Galaxies Beyond Galaxies: The Discoveries Of Edwin Hubble 53

The Lab Mistake That Gave Us Penicillin 54

That Time Benjamin Franklin Electrocuted A Turkey..., And
Himself!...56

Jonathan Swift And The Moons Of Mars............................57

How Isaac Newton Split Light Into The Spectrum....................58

Archimedes' Bathtub 59

Did You Know? 61

NATURE.. 62

The Shark That Lived For 500 Years 63

Feathered Dinosaurs?...64

The Bird That Takes On The World's Longest Migration 66

The Witches' Wind: Argentina's Disheartening Weather
Phenomenon 68

The Pitohui: The World's Only Poisonous Bird 70

Carlos Jared And The Venomous Frogs Of The Amazon 71

How Owls Fly So Quietly 73

The Last Thylacine 74

Did You Know? 75

MYSTERIES 76

The Curse Of King Tut's Tomb 77

The Bermuda Triangle 79

The Crimes Of Jack The Ripper 81

What Is Stonehenge For? 82

The Loch Ness Monster 83

The Disappearance Of The *Mary Celeste* 84

Amelia Earhart's Last Flight 85

The Roanoke Disappearances 87

Did You Know? 88

KINGS & QUEENS 89

The Time Henry Viii Wrestled Against The King Of France 90

The Madness Of King George 92

The King Who Thought He Was Made Of Glass 94

The Princes In The Tower 95

Henry Iii's *White Ship* Disaster 96

Maria Eleonora, The Madcap Queen Of Sweden 98

Mustafa I, The Sultan Who Lived In A Cage (Twice!)..................99

Queen Victoria, The Grandmother Of Europe.............................. 101

Did You Know? 102

SPORTS & GAMES 103

Jesse Owens' Record Breaking 45 Minutes...............................104

When The Olympic Games Became Crafty!...............................105

Gaylord Perry And The Men On The Moon 107

How To Shuffle A Pack Of Cards...108

The Miracle On Ice...109

The Longest Tennis Game In History 110

Harry Chiti: The MLB Player Who Was Traded For Himself 111

The World's Oldest Chess Set 112

Did You Know? 113

LITERATURE & THE ARTS.................................... 114

The Shipwreck That Inspired Shakespeare............................... 115

Charles Dickens' Life On Stage 117

The Americans Of American Gothic 118

The Game That Gave Us Frankenstein..................................... 119

The Man Who Stole The Mona Lisa 121

The Man Behind Sherlock Holmes 123

Van Gogh's Only Sale..124

How A Christmas Carol Was A Dickensian Disaster 125

Did You Know? 127

MEDICINE 128

A Plague Of Dancing 129

Chang And Eng Bunker: The Conjoined Twins Who Captivated The World..........130

How The Artificial Heart Changed The Medical World..........131

The World's First Blood Bank..........132

And The World's First Vaccine..........133

Babies' Bones: How Human Skeletons Are Formed *After* We Are Born!..........135

The Philosopher Who Laughed Himself To Death..........136

Julius Caesar And The Caesarean Section..........137

Did You Know? 138

EXPLORATION..........139

Captain Cook's Last Voyage..........140

"The Worst Journey In The World"..........142

A Trip To The South Pole..........143

Shackleton's Lost Ship..........144

The Man Who Vanished In The Australian Bush..........146

Gudrid Thorbjarnardóttir: The First Female Explorer Of The New World..........147

The Explorer Who Gave His Name To America..........148

The Darien Scheme: Scotland's Failed Attempt At A New World Colony..........149

Did You Know? 151

DISASTERS..........152

The London Tornado Of 1091..........153

The Great Molasses Flood..........154

The Tunguska Event..........155

The Eruption Of Krakatoa 156

The Year Without A Summer 157

The Lake Nyos Disaster 158

The Pepsi Juice Flood 159

The Day It Rained Golf Balls 160

Did You Know? 161

GENERAL KNOWLEDGE 162

The Child Who Gave Us A "Googol"................................163

Why Sandwiches Are Called...Sandwiches! 164

The Man Who Bought Alaska.......................................165

The Bear That Lived At The Tower Of London...............166

The Dog That Ate Steinbeck's Masterpiece 167

The World's First Skyscraper 168

Toy Story 2: The Movie That Was Almost Lost............169

Daniel Bakeman: The Last Survivor Of The Revolutionary
War 170

Did You Know? 171

CONCLUSION 172

INTRODUCTION

Have you heard of someone called Queen Maria Eleonora of Sweden?

How about Harry Chiti, Ignacio Anaya, or Daniel F Bakeman?

Or how about this - have you heard of the New Guinea pitohui? Or Greening's venomous tree frog?

Have you heard of the shipwreck of the Sea Venture? Or the first mother to travel to North America? Or the tornado that destroyed medieval London?

Don't worry if the answer to any of those questions is no..., because that's precisely where this book comes in!

You might not have heard of any of those people, creatures, or extraordinary events, but behind every one of them is a super interesting story - and there are dozens of amazing tales just like them in *Super Interesting Stories For Curious Kids*!

Inside this book are more than 100 stories covering everything from famous people from history to bizarre weather, amazing animals, peculiar unsolved mysteries, and remarkable scientific discoveries. And what all of these stories have in common is that they are all *super interesting*!

All of the stories here have been divided into themed sections, beginning with history. So, you can either dive right in with our first story over the page here or flick back to the contents page to start in whatever section takes your fancy! Regardless of how you choose to use this book, though, you can rest assured that all the tales here are *super interesting*!

HISTORY

THAT TIME ABRAHAM LINCOLN FOUGHT A DUEL

It was way back in August 1842 that the future president of the United States, Abraham Lincoln, wrote a rude letter criticizing a political rival named James Shields, and had it published in a local newspaper in Illinois - under the fake name "Rebecca"! A few days later, Lincoln's then-girlfriend, and his future First Lady, Mary Todd, wrote her own letter criticizing Shields and had that published under the fake name "Cathleen" too. Understandably, Shields was not happy with the couple's letters and the public criticism, so he contacted the editor of the newspaper to find out who the real authors of the letters were. Once he had tracked them down, Shields challenged Lincoln to a sword-fighting duel to settle their differences.

At the time, dueling was illegal in Illinois, and so the pair would have to cross the border into Missouri. They met for their duel at a place known as Bloody Island a few weeks later. Standing on either side of a plank of wood - which the rules of the fight demanded they do not cross - the pair took up their weapons and stepped forward to begin the duel. At six feet four inches tall, however, Lincoln towered several inches over Shields' head. As he prepared for the fight to start, Lincoln swung his sword high and in doing so accidentally cut right through the bough of a tree that was growing above where the two men stood. As the branch crashed to the ground, Lincoln and Shields' friends - who had come to watch and support them in their fight - stepped in from the sidelines and ended the fight before it had a chance to begin. The two men quickly called a truce and went their separate ways.

As luck would have it, however, two decades later the pair had the chance to end their disagreement once and for all. By now, Lincoln was the president and Shields was a Brigadier General in the Union Army of the Potomac during the American Civil War. Shields excelled in combat before being injured badly while fighting at the Battle of Kernstown on March 23, 1862. In recognition of his contribution to the Union side's victory at the battle, Lincoln put Shields forward for promotion to the rank of Major General, and in doing so, ended the years-long disagreement between the two men.

THE YEAR OF THE FOUR EMPERORS

The Roman emperor Nero is one of the most famous and bizarre leaders in Roman history. In the 14 years in which he ruled over the Roman Empire - from the year CE 54 until CE 68 - Nero had several of his friends and family members imprisoned, had his mother Agrippina murdered, and is famously said to have simply played music while the city of Rome burned down around him. There is even a rumor that Nero himself started the fire that eventually destroyed the city!

On Nero's death in CE 68, Rome was thrown into 12 months of turmoil in which a chain of equally curious leaders ruled in quick succession. This extraordinary time has since become known as "The Year of the Four Emperors."

At first, Nero was followed by a new emperor, named Galba, who remained in power for the next seven months. Like Nero before him, however, Galba's reign quickly became violent and unpredictable, and he too soon gained a reputation for having anyone in his senate who disagreed with him killed. When his popularity plummeted, Galba was assassinated by a fellow Roman leader named Otho, who took over where he left off.

Galba's rule had been so bad, though, that some regions of the Roman Empire had turned their back on Rome altogether and appointed their own local leaders instead. And one of these - the ruler of a province called Germania, named Aulus Vitellius - now wanted to be emperor of all Rome. He marched his armies south from Germany to Italy, defeated Otho in battle, and was quickly swept into power. But just a few weeks later, another regional leader named Vespasian decided that he wanted to do the same.

Vespasian had risen to lead some of the provinces in the east of the Roman Empire. In December CE 69, he marched his armies westwards in an attack on Rome, overthrew Vitellius, and took control of Rome as the year came to an end. Happily, Vespasian proved a good and just leader, and quickly set about restoring some much -needed peace and stability to the empire.

FRANZ FERDINAND ESCAPED ONE ASSASSINATION ATTEMPT... ONLY TO FALL INTO ANOTHER!

You might not have heard of Archduke Franz Ferdinand, but you will have heard of what happened after he was murdered in 1914: it was his death that led to the commencement of World War I.

At the time of his death, Franz Ferdinand was the heir to an important empire in the middle of Europe known as the Austro-Hungarian Empire. The empire covered a huge amount of central Europe. It extended far beyond the modern countries of Austria and Hungary themselves. Franz Ferdinand's family - led by his father, the ruling Archduke Karl Ludwig - had power over much of what is now modern-day Romania, Poland, the Czech Republic, Slovakia, Slovenia, Croatia, Bosnia, and Serbia. Franz Ferdinand himself was destined one day to succeed his father and come to control this vast area himself - but as it happened, he would not survive long enough to do so...

Like many empires throughout history, some of the regions over which the Austro-Hungarian Empire had control were not happy and wished instead to be independent countries. Protests against the archduke's rule and plots to get rid of him and his family were therefore common across the empire. In Summer 1914, the young Archduke Franz Ferdinand was told that he should cancel an upcoming visit to the Bosnian capital of Sarajevo for fear of an attempt on his life. Franz Ferdinand, however, was determined to carry out the visit. He and his wife arrived in the city on June 28. Shortly after, as the archduke's car trundled through the busy streets, a protestor in the crowd threw a bomb at his vehicle in an attempt to blow it up! But the would-be assassin failed, and the bomb simply bounced off the car's roof, fell under another vehicle behind it, and exploded on the ground, blasting a huge crater into the roadway.

The archduke and his wife were understandably shaken up by the attempt on their lives and hurried to their destination. Once they had recovered, however, the archduke was confident that having survived the assassination attempt they would now be safe in the city. Tragically, he was wrong, and as their car made its way to their next destination in the city, another assassin - a Serbian young man of just 19, named Gavrilo Princip - ran forward from the crowd and fired a gun into the archduke's car, killing both him and his wife.

In the aftermath of the assassination, Austria-Hungary declared war on Princip's home nation of Serbia, and as other countries joined the fight the conflict steadily grew and grew. Before long, almost all the countries of Europe - as well as many others around the world, including the United States - had been drawn into the war. Despite surviving one attempt on his life, Franz Ferdinand's death in another just a matter of hours later eventually drew much of the world into World War I.

FIDEL CASTRO'S EXPLODING CIGAR

Fidel Castro was a famous leader of the Caribbean island of Cuba. Having been born on the island in 1926, Castro was imprisoned in 1953 following his involvement in a series of violent rebellions aimed at overthrowing the Cuban government. After his release from jail, he fled to Mexico and there began to assemble a band of revolutionary supporters. He returned to Cuba with these supporters in the late 1950s and swept to power in 1959.

Having claimed the presidency of Cuba as his own - without holding an election or following the rules of democracy - Castro immediately stirred up anger in the United States. America's politicians became worried that having an unpredictable leader just offshore was a very risky situation. As a result, America soon began taking steps to have Castro removed from power, and a new government put in place that the United States could live and work alongside in peace. All America's attempts to remove Castro failed, however - including one very bizarre plot in the mid-1960s!

The story goes that Fidel Castro was very fond of smoking cigars. The CIA ultimately planned to use an exploding cigar in an attempt to assassinate him. When Castro lit the stogie, it would explode violently, killing him instantly and paving the way for a replacement president!

The truth of this plot has been the subject of rumor ever since, with some historians claiming that it was never a serious plan and is nothing more than an urban legend. There was, however, a very real plan put in place in 1960 to deliver a box of poisoned cigars to Castro while he was visiting the United Nations in New York. So, if the CIA were willing to give the Cuban leader toxic cigars, maybe the plot to give him exploding cigars really was genuine as well!

THE PURITANS WHO BANNED CHRISTMAS

The Puritans were a very devout group of people who, hundreds of years ago, followed an extremely strict and intensely Christian lifestyle. If you have heard of them before, it has probably been in stories of the early European settlers who arrived in America in the 1600s. It was groups of Puritans that came on board ships like the Mayflower, as they fled from England the Europe in the hopes of establishing new devout communities for themselves in the New World.

Although some Puritans left England for America in the early 1600s, many remained behind. They tried to live a devout life in Europe and put new strict religious laws in place there. And in 1644, one group of English Puritans in particular did just that, when they succeeded in banning people from celebrating Christmas!

At that time, a Puritan leader named Oliver Cromwell had swept to power in England and overthrown the king, Charles I. Under Cromwell's rule, a raft of new Christian laws had been imposed on England, and in 1644, Cromwell passed an Act of Parliament that outlawed Christmas.

The Puritans disliked Christmas because they saw its fun and festivities as a threat to the holiday's Christian teachings and lifestyle. Playing games, singing carols, and eating and drinking too much were all seen as wasteful and ungodly acts by the Puritans. That is why they outlawed the festive holiday altogether in an attempt to return it to its religious roots. Cromwell's government even made it illegal to eat mince pies!

In the end, however, the Puritans' war on Christmas failed. The festive period proved so popular that despite the new laws, many people continued to celebrate the holiday in secret and so the Christmas traditions endured. The ban on Christmas merrymaking was eventually lifted in 1660 - two years after Cromwell's death, and the same year that Charles I's eldest surviving son took his place as King Charles II.

THE DEAD POPE WHO WAS PUT ON TRIAL!

When he was elected pope in 2013, Pope Francis incredibly became the 266th person to hold the title of head of the Catholic church in almost 2,000 years of its history. The very first pope was Saint Peter, who held the title of Bishop of Rome (as it was at the time) way back in the 1st century CE.

In those 2,000 years, however, some very strange characters have held the title of pope, and some very strange popes have been involved in some very strange occurrences indeed! And perhaps none is more peculiar than the so-called Cadaver Synod, when in the late 800s CE, the ruling pope, Stephen VI, had the dead body of the preceding pope, Formosus, dug up and put on trial in a religious court!

Pope Formosus was a controversial figure who ruled over the Catholic church for just five years, from 891 until his death in 896. At that point, Pope Stephen VI took over, but some in the church objected to Stephen's appointment. Looking for a way of drawing a line under Formosus' reign and reinforcing his own, Stephen demanded that - more than seven months after his death - Formosus' body should be dug up from its grave, brought before him in a Catholic courtroom, and made to answer questions about Formosus' time as pope. Stephen's orders were carried out, and in January 897, Formosus' body was placed in a courtroom dock in the Vatican and quizzed by Pope Stephen and his followers. (Unable to answer the questions asked of it, of course, a Vatican deacon answered on Formosus' behalf!)

The verdict of Stephen's court was that Formosus was guilty of several crimes. His time as pope was therefore struck from the papal records and sentenced to be executed. Formosus already being dead, of course, the execution could not be carried out all too effectively - so instead, his body was simply dumped in Rome's river Tiber!

THE DESTRUCTION OF POMPEII

Surely one of the most famous events in European history is the eruption of Mount Vesuvius in CE 79, which caused the utter destruction of the Ancient Roman cities of Pompeii and Herculaneum, in southern Italy.

At the time of the disaster, Pompeii was a bustling city of around 20,000 people. Nearby Herculaneum - - though smaller, and home to only around a quarter of that number - was a coastal resort town, popular among rich Roman citizens. Both cities were wealthy and prosperous areas, but their growth came to a sudden end at noon on August 24, CE 79, when one of the biggest volcanoes in Europe, Mount Vesuvius, began to erupt after centuries of lying dormant.

The eruption was immense, with almost the entire top of the volcano blasting open and throwing tons of ash, gas, stone, and dust around ten miles into the air. Then an enormous quantity of molten hot material began to rain down on the surrounding towns over the next 12 hours. Most of the people in Pompeii and Herculaneum fled, but perhaps as many as 2,000 of them remained behind in their homes, attics, and basements, hoping to wait out the eruption and escape once the volcano had calmed down. Unfortunately, few, if any of them, survived.

In the afternoon, a sudden change in wind direction forced a boiling hot cloud of gas and toxic vapors to blow down directly onto Herculaneum, killing all of the people who remained there. It was followed by a mudslide, which buried the entire town under several feet of volcanic earth and rock. Although Pompeii at first escaped the same fate as its neighboring town, early the following morning, on August 25, a second toxic cloud of material was blown down the volcanic mountainside directly at the city. All those who were still in Pompeii were killed instantly, before a second fall of ash and dust covered the remains of the town, in places up to a depth of 17 feet!

The disaster was so utterly complete that in the aftermath the Romans made no attempt to recover or rebuild their lost towns, and both Pompeii and Herculaneum were abandoned. The towns' precise locations were eventually forgotten, and it was not until the 1700s that some of their remains were uncovered, entirely by chance. Since then, archeologists and historians have continued to dig up both sites. Today tourists visiting southern Italy can wander around the long-forgotten streets of Pompeii and Herculaneum - and can even look at the stony preserved remains of some of the people who tragically lost their lives in the disaster almost 2,000 years ago!

RA, RA, RASPUTIN!

Have you heard of the Russian monk Rasputin?

He is one of the most famous and most bizarre figures in Russian history, who for several decades worked his way into the favor of the Russian royal family - until his downfall and eventual murder in some very bizarre circumstances indeed!

Grigori Rasputin was born in Pokrovskoye, a town close to Russia's border with Kazakhstan, in 1869. Leaving behind a troubled childhood, Rasputin joined a monastery when he was just a teenager and began training as a monk. Within a year, however, Rasputin had abandoned his religious training and instead embarked on the life of a peasant, wandering across much of Siberia, western Russia, and eastern Europe. His peculiar religious views began to earn him a reputation as a mystical healer, soothsayer, and hypnotist.

Eventually, Rasputin's wanderings took him to the city of St. Petersburg, in northern Russia, where his reputation as a magical healer led to him being introduced to the Russian royal family. At the time, the young son of the ruler of Russia, Tsar Nicholas, was ill with a blood disorder (hemophilia). Rasputin apparently used his hypnotic powers to calm the boy down, and in doing so, he impressed the tsar with his mystical abilities.

Fearing for his son's health if Rasputin were ever to leave, Nicholas kept him around his court - but outside of the royal court, Rasputin's behavior was terrible, and he made a great many enemies. During World War I, meanwhile, Rasputin served as an advisor to the Russian ruler, but all his decisions proved bad and his involvement in the tsar's court became ever more unpopular. Eventually, a plot was hatched to have Rasputin murdered and end his influence on Russian politics.

On the night of December 29, 1916, Rasputin was invited to the home of Prince Feliks Yusupov, the husband of Tsar Nicholas' niece. There, he was served poisoned cakes and wine. Bizarrely, the mystical monk seemed completely unharmed by the poisoned platter, so Prince Feliks had to resort to more violent methods and took up his gun and shot Rasputin in the chest. Even still, however, he did not die!

Incredibly, Rasputin ran from Feliks' home and outside was shot once again, this time by Vladimir Purishkevich, a member of the Russian parliament who was also in on the plot. When even Purishkevich's bullet failed to bring Rasputin down, he was set upon by a gang of men who bound his hands and feet and threw him in the freezing River Nevka in St. Petersburg, where he drowned.

Rasputin's hold on the Russian royal family was at long last over - though some have claimed that his final act was to curse all those he left behind. The following year, there was a revolution in Russia, and the entire royal family was overthrown and murdered!

DID YOU KNOW?

○ The Leaning Tower of Pisa has NEVER been straight - it started leaning while it was still being built!

○ Cleopatra's real name was Cleopatra VII Thea Philopator - literally meaning "father-loving goddess"!

○ The shortest war in history was fought between Britain and the tiny African island of Zanzibar. It lasted just 38 minutes!

○ Adolf Hitler was once nominated for the Nobel Peace Prize!

○ Oxford University was founded in 1096 before the Aztecs began their empire in 1428.

○ The Ancient Greeks believed people with red hair became vampires after their death!

○ Albert Einstein was once offered the chance to become president of Israel - but he turned the offer down.

SCIENCE

THE BIG BANG IS STILL WARMING THE UNIVERSE!

Today, the Big Bang is the principal theory explaining the origin of our universe.

Most scientists now believe that the universe began in an enormous outward explosion from a single dense central point. In simple terms, everything in the universe was originally held in this one spot, but there was so much matter, light, and energy in this one space that it was very unstable. Eventually - around 13.8 billion years ago! - This single point exploded in a violent burst of energy and activity. Everything in the universe was at that point suddenly thrown outward, and the universe has been continuing to expand and stretch ever since.

The Big Bang Theory, as it is now known, was first proposed in the 1920s by an astronomer called Georges Lemaître. His idea was later shown to be true by the American astronomer Edwin Hubble, who used powerful telescopes to look further into outer space. Hubble found that some of the stars and galaxies surrounding our own are moving away from us - with those furthest away from us moving faster than those closer to us. His discovery proved the universe is expanding; and if everything is still expanding today, then we can presume that everyone was once a lot closer together - in a single spot!

As the universe has continued to expand, however, it has continued to cool (and will, according to some scientists at least, continue to cool until the end of time!). But incredibly, some of the heat produced by the Big Bang all those billions of years ago can still be felt in the universe, as something called the universe's cosmic microwave background, or CMB.

CMB is a form of radiation left over from the explosion of the Big Bang. You cannot see this invisible radiation, but it can be measured - and when the first television sets were produced in the early 1900s, CMB used to cause the static "fuzz" that appeared on the screen if the television was not tuned to a station correctly!
Taxicab Numbers: the Story Behind Math's Most Amazing Digits

TAXICAB NUMBERS: THE STORY BEHIND MATH'S MOST AMAZING DIGITS

Do you know what a prime number is?

If you know a lot about math, you might have heard of prime numbers before. These are figures that can only be divided equally by themselves, and the number 1. So, the number 7 is a prime number, for instance, because it can only be divided by itself ($7 \div 7 = 1$) or by the number 1 ($7 \div 1 = 7$). The number 8, however, is not prime because it can be equally divided by 2 ($8 \div 2 = 4$) and 4 ($8 \div 4 = 2$) as well as itself ($8 \div 8 = 1$) and 1 ($8 \div 1 = 8$).

But prime numbers are not the only kind of number that mathematicians have identified like this. In fact, they have all sorts of names for different numbers and number groups that share strange qualities and peculiarities like this in common. Square numbers, for instance, are the product of a number multiplied by itself, like 9 (= 3 x 3) and 16 (= 4 x 4). Cube numbers are numbers multiplied by themselves three times, like 27 (= 3 x 3 x 3). And then there is a very peculiar set of numbers called "taxicabs."

A taxicab number is a number that can be made by adding together two different cube numbers in two different ways. Aside from the number 1 (which is the sum of $1^3 + 1^3$), the lowest taxicab number is actually quite big - it is 1,789, which is the sum of both $1^3 + 12^3$ and $9^3 + 10^3$. Numbers like this are very rare; in fact, there is not another taxicab number after 1,789 until you reach 87,539,319! But all of this mind-boggling math aside, there is still one very good question here: why are these figures known as taxicabs?

It was in the late 1910s that a British mathematician named GH Hardy traveled from his home in Cambridge to visit his friend, fellow mathematician Srinivasa Ramanujan, who was in hospital in London. The number of the taxi Hardy took to the hospital was 1789, which he happened to mention to Ramanujan did not strike him as a particularly interesting number. Ramanujan, however, was quick to correct him. Far from being uninteresting, 1,789, he pointed out, "is a very interesting number: it is the smallest number expressible as the sum of two cubes in two different ways!" The Seeds That Went Into Space

Human beings have been sending things into space - including other human beings! - Since the 1940s and 1950s. In the early days of space travel, nothing more than unmanned space probes and satellites were sent beyond the limits of the Earth's atmosphere (with some missions proving more successful than others). But as time went by and technology improved, some early experiments began sending animals into space - including several mice, ants, rabbits, more than 30 monkeys in total, and the famous space dog Laika, who was sent into outer space by the Soviet Union in 1957.

The first human in space, the Russian cosmonaut Yuri Gagarin, followed on board the *Vostok 1* space craft in 1961, before NASA and the United States landed the first humans on the surface of the Moon in 1969. Some of the very earliest living things to travel into space, however, were not animals or human beings at all, but plants.

Way back in 1946, the United States launched several types of seeds - including maize, cotton, and rye - into space before returning them safely to Earth. The aim was to investigate whether leaving the Earth's atmosphere would affect their growth. To the surprise of the early NASA researchers, the seeds were not damaged at all by their journey into space. Twenty years later, in 1966, things went one step further when the Russian spacecraft

Kosmos 110 was launched with a parcel of seeds on board - including lettuce seeds and cabbage seeds - that managed to germinate in space, becoming the first foodstuffs ever grown in outer space. And finally, in 1971, NASA sent no less than 500 tree seeds into space on board the *Apollo 14* mission. The seeds, which included sycamore, redwood, and Douglas fir trees - orbited the Moon before being safely returned to Earth and planted by the US Forestry Service. Incredibly, these seeds suffered no ill effects from their lunar journey, and several of these so-called "Moon Trees" are still growing in various locations across the United States!

DMITRI MENDELEEV
AND THE ORGANIZATION
OF THE ELEMENTS

If you like science, you might have heard of the periodic table of elements.

Elements are the fundamental substances of science. From gases and metals to liquids and highly radioactive man-made substances, more than 100 elements have so far been identified and discovered. The periodic table is a diagram of all these elements, which organizes the basic chemical building blocks of our world into a vast chart, ranking each one by its atomic number - that is, the number of protons, or positive particles, in the nucleus of each element's atom. Element number one, for instance, is hydrogen, as a single atom of hydrogen gas has just a single proton.

The idea of arranging all the known elements into a table dates back around three hundred years. In the mid-1700s, several scientists tried to arrange all the elements that they knew of, at the time, into tables. Some early periodic tables organized the elements into groups of three sharing similar atomic weight, and groups of eight. Scientists using these early tables began to see patterns in the arrangement of the elements too. Those in each set of eight, the British chemist John Newlands found, had very similar properties compared to those in the next row or set of eight. But these early tables were not perfect, and they contained many mistakes and inconsistencies for one very good reason: not all of the elements we know of today had been discovered yet!

It was not until 1869 that a Russian chemist named Dmitri Mendeleev put together the first periodic table as we know it today, leaving gaps for elements he rightly predicted must exist, but which had not yet been discovered or created. Ordering the elements by atomic weight - but leaving spaces for numbers that could not yet be filled - meant that Mendeleev's periodic table was incomplete but perfectly accurate.

Mendeleev even went so far as to give some of these undiscovered elements names: element number 31, for instance, he gave the name "eka-aluminum," as it was listed directly below aluminum on his period table, and so would likely share some of its properties. When element number 31 was discovered in 1875 - and renamed "gallium" - it was indeed found to be a relatively soft, silvery aluminum-like metal, just as Mendeleev had predicted!

WHY DOES URANUS SPIN ON ITS SIDE?

There are seven other planets in our solar system: Mercury and Venus lie closer to the Sun than the Earth, while moving out from the Earth on the opposite side, away from the Sun, lie Mars, Jupiter, Saturn, Uranus, and Neptune.

These planets have some interesting and very peculiar properties. Saturn, for instance, is famous for its rings - but the biggest planet, Jupiter, also has a ring system that is so thin it is barely visible from Earth. Venus, meanwhile, has such a perilous atmosphere that despite being further from the Sun than its neighbor Mercury, it is the hottest planet in the solar system. While all the other planets rotate counter-clockwise, meanwhile, Venus is the only one to rotate clockwise - while even more bizarrely, the planet Uranus rotates on its side!

In fact, Uranus rotates at an angle of almost 90 degrees from upright, so that while all the other planets in the solar system - including our own! - A appear to move around the Sun on a flat plane, Uranus appears more like a rolling ball, turning and rotating over itself as it completes its orbit.

Precisely why Uranus has such a peculiar rotation has been the subject of debate among astronomers for decades, ever since Uranus was first discovered in 1781. Today, the most common theory is that early in the development of our solar system, a gigantic space rock - perhaps as large as the Earth itself - likely bumped into Uranus, knocking it from its upright position and sending it off around the Sun at its present 90-degree angle.

No matter the cause of this bizarre tilt, Uranus' position means that it has the most extreme seasons of any planet, as each of its poles is at some point in its orbit pointed directly at the Sun. Because it takes Uranus a full 84 years to complete a single circuit of the Sun, however, this means that at the height of summer on Uranus the Sun would not set in the sky for 21 years - while on the opposite side of the planet, plunged into the depth of Uranus' winter, the Sun would not rise for the same two decades!

BANANAS ARE RADIOACTIVE!

Bananas are very good for you. Full of natural sugar, yet containing only around 100 calories each, a ripe banana is also a good source of dietary fiber and minerals. But despite their obvious health benefits, bananas have another very peculiar quality: they are very faintly radioactive!

Radioactivity is a form of radiation that we might normally associate with dangerous chemicals, rocks, and minerals such as plutonium and uranium. High levels of this kind of radioactivity - the kind given out by hazardous substances like these - can indeed be very dangerous to human life and can make a person very, very sick. It might be surprising, then, to find out that something as simple and as apparently healthy as a banana is radioactive as well. So how does that happen? And how dangerous is a banana?!

Bananas are radioactive because they contain a relatively large amount of a metal and dietary mineral called potassium. Our bodies need potassium to help keep us hydrated and our energy levels replenished - but all potassium is very faintly radioactive, and bananas have it in such high amounts that the bananas themselves, in turn, give off a very small amount of radioactive radiation.

If this sounds dangerous, and makes it seem like you should start dropping bananas from your diet, don't worry! Although bananas contain large amounts of potassium, the levels of radioactivity in potassium are so low that it is effectively completely harmless. In fact, you would need to eat around 200 bananas in a single sitting to receive the same amount of radiation as your body undergoes when you get an x-ray in the hospital!

ISAAC NEWTON'S APPLE

Besides radioactive bananas, another fruit that has taken quite an important role in the world of science is the apple that fell on Sir Isaac Newton's head to give him the idea behind his theories of gravity - according to legend, at least!

Born in England in 1642, Sir Isaac Newton is one of the world's greatest-ever scientific minds. His life's work covered all kinds of different subjects, including mathematics, astronomy, chemistry, optics, and physics - but it is for his work on gravity, and the groundbreaking theories he devised around it, that he is perhaps best-known today. And according to one of the most famous stories in all scientific history, we can thank an apple tree in Newton's garden for giving him these extraordinary ideas!

According to the tale, Newton had been mulling over his scientific theories around the Earth's gravitational pull for several days when he happened to sit beneath an apple tree on the grounds of his home, Woolsthorpe Manor, in the English county of Lincolnshire. As he sat there, the tree shed one of its apples, which fell - under the influence of gravity - onto Newton's head. The bump was all Newton needed, and he leaped from beneath the tree, ran back inside and into his laboratory, and began work on what would eventually become his Universal Laws of Motion and Gravitation.

As famous as this story is, however, how true it really is remains something of a mystery. No record of the tale is recorded in any of Newton's own notebooks, but both he and his niece, Catherine Barton, later related versions of the story to friends and fellow scientists. Although countless different versions of this tale exist, at least one part of it appears not to be true: the apple unfortunately did not land on Newton's head!

The more likely version of this story is that Newton was only watching the tree in his garden when an apple happened to fall from it, and inspired by the simple drop of a piece of fruit from a tree's branches, he set to work coming up with the formulas about the Earth's gravity that would go on to change the world of science forever. So, part of the story may be a myth, but the tree itself is still standing in Newton's Garden today! Albert Einstein's Missing Brain

Almost 300 years after Isaac Newton's theories of gravity were first put forward, they went on to inspire another of the scientific world's greatest minds: Albert Einstein. In the early 1900s, Einstein was formulating his famous theories of relativity, a major part of which rested on our understanding of Newton's theories of gravity.

Einstein went on to win the Nobel Prize for Physics in 1921, and over the course of the 20th century, became one of the world's most renowned and recognized scientists. When he died at the age of 76 in 1955, the scientific world had lost a true genius, the likes of which would perhaps never be seen again. But the gap Einstein's death left in the scientific world led at least one of the scientists at Princeton Hospital, where Einstein died, to do something rather bizarre.

After Einstein's death, the surgeon on call at the hospital, Dr. Thomas Stoltz Harvey, carried out an autopsy on Einstein's body to determine the cause of his death. In doing his analysis, however, Harvey removed Einstein's brain from his body - without the permission of his family - and cut it into over 200 pieces. He placed samples on glass microscope plates and put them in his store at the hospital in the hope that scientists in the future could work out what it was about Einstein's brain that had made him so intelligent. The rest of Einstein's body was cremated, and his ashes scattered in New Jersey, but Einstein's stolen brain - cut up into blocks and prepared for future analysis - remained among Harvey's belongings at Princeton.

As the decades passed by, Einstein's brain remained in store until Harvey left the hospital and took it with him when he retired and moved to Wichita, Kansas. A local journalist tracked Harvey down to his home 23 years after Einstein's death and asked him about Einstein's brain, which Harvey showed to the journalist - kept inside a beer cooler!

When the story of Einstein's brain broke in the news, Harvey was suddenly made famous. In 1985, he came out of retirement and carried out the very first analysis of the brain in its history. Harvey effectively stealing the brain from Einstein's body may not have been entirely above board, to say the least, but when the analysis was published it gave us a new insight into the biological side of human intelligence.

DID YOU KNOW?

○ Tin has the shortest name of any element on the periodic table.

○ Asteroids can have rings and moons just like planets can!

○ The oceans produce more oxygen than the world's trees.

○ The Earth travels around the Sun at around 67,000 miles per hour!

○ 99.9% of everyone's DNA is the same.

○ If you were to fly to the Sun in a normal airplane, it would take you 20 years!

○ Light is so quick it travels nearly 186,412 miles in a single second!

INVENTIONS

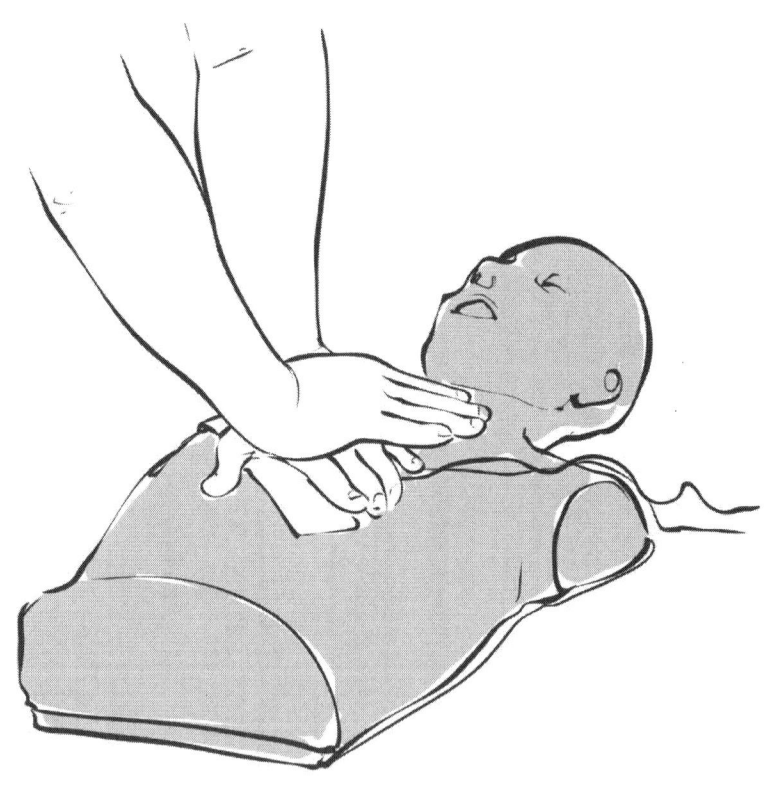

HEDY LAMARR:
THE HOLLYWOOD STAR
TURNED INVENTOR

She might not be a household name in the world today, but in her heyday in the 1930s and 40s, Hedy Lamarr was one of the most famous and admired actresses in all of Hollywood. The star of classic movies like *Algiers*, *Boom Town*, and *Samson and Delilah*, Lamarr's career on the screen spanned three decades until her retirement from the movies - and her eventual disappearance into a life of quiet seclusion - in the late 1950s. But alongside her movie career, one of Hollywood's most famous starlets had a surprising second string to her bow: she was an inventor.

Although she had no training or education as a scientist, Lamarr was amazed by scientific advances and inventions. Between takes and rehearsals on set during her movie career, she would reportedly spend her time designing new and improved devices and machines. Then, at the height of her career in the late 1930s, Lamarr had the opportunity to put her talents to good use with the outbreak of World War II.

Lamarr's husband at the time was a weapons expert and arms dealer, and she learned through one of his business associates that the American Navy needed a way of guiding torpedoes through the water after they had been fired. Radio control technology was still relatively new in the 1930s and 40s, and radio signals could be jammed or interfered with by the enemy (making it possible that an enemy ship or submarine could even turn a torpedo back around on the vessel that had fired it!).

Lamarr, however, had an idea: if the radio signal controlling the torpedo was constantly and unpredictably changing frequencies, then the enemy craft would not be able to match it and interfere with it! That would prevent the weapon from being jammed. Working with a friend of hers, the Hollywood writer and composer George Antheil, who was also interested in inventions and new technology, Lamarr developed a system of "frequency hopping." With Antheil's help, she patented a device that could do just that in 1941.

As it happens, Lamarr's extraordinarily innovative idea has gone on to have long-lasting importance: today, a similar technology is used in Bluetooth communication, GPS, and is even used to prevent Wi-Fi internet signals from being hacked or tapped into!

THE DUTCH SAILORS
WHO INVENTED BRANDY

Brandy is a strong alcoholic drink with a burnt brown color and an often woody or smoky taste. It is made by putting wine through a chemical process known as distillation, in which a liquid is boiled to produce a vapor, and then cooled to turn the vapor back into a liquid, removing sharpness and impurities along the way.

This process of turning wine into distilled brandy was first developed in France in the 1300s. Back then, the resulting drink was originally considered more of a medicine than a beverage, and so was used more as a restorative tonic or liquor that could help ailing patients regain their strength and vitality. Some French doctors who prescribed brandy to their patients even went so far as to label it *l'eau de vie*, or "the water of life."

Brandy continued to be seen as a medicinal liquor for the next few hundred years, until a happy accident on board an unnamed Dutch merchant's ship in the early 1600s. According to the story, the merchant in question wished to transport large quantities of wine in barrels on board his ship and came up with an ingenious plan that would allow him to carry more wine in less space: he set about heating the wine up.

Boiling the wine in enormous vats led to much of its water content being evaporated and the liquid itself becoming more concentrated. It is much like a chef or a home cook reducing a soup or stew on a stovetop! With the liquid now taking up less space and less weight than before, even more of it could be transported on board the ship. All that the merchant had to do when he arrived at this destination was mix fresh water back into the concentrated wine, replacing the liquid that had been lost.

As it happens, however, boiling the wine in this way not only reduced its water content but concentrated and purified its flavor similar to how distilling the wine had all those centuries earlier. The barrels of concentrated wine ultimately proved popular as a drink on their own—with the extra water added in—and were sold under the Dutch name *brandewijn*, literally meaning "burnt wine!"

THE KITCHEN MISHAP
THAT GAVE US CORN FLAKES

Today, Corn Flakes are one of the world's most popular breakfast cereals. Light, nutritious, and tasty, millions of boxes of the cereal are sold every year globally, while the brand Kellogg's Corn Flakes in particular - with its famous rooster logo - is one of the most recognizable food brands in the world. But despite being a breakfast staple practically everywhere, amazingly this famous cereal was invented entirely by accident.

It was back in the 1870s that two brothers, John, and William Kellogg, took over the management of a specialized hospital or sanitarium in Battle Creek, Michigan. There, the brothers promoted the health benefits of a good diet, and they set about inventing and testing new foods and dishes to give to their patients.

One of the brother's experiments involved making a nutritious pastry-like mash out of boiled wheat. One day, however, the brothers left a batch of the boiled wheat dough out on a countertop in the hospital's kitchen overnight. When they tried to roll it out, the dried dough began to break apart into tiny flakes. Unsure of what to do with what they thought was little more than a spoiled batch of dough, the brothers lightly toasted the dough flakes in the oven - and to their surprise, accidentally created a light, nutritious cereal.

The new food proved a hit with the Kellogg brothers' patients, and after they began marketing their accidental invention publicly, they soon began selling thousands of pounds of the wheat flakes every year. Kellogg's Corn Flakes, as they became known, have been a popular breakfast cereal ever since!

WHY DID EARLY CHAMPAGNE BOTTLES KEEP EXPLODING?

If you've ever seen a bottle of champagne being opened, you might have seen the rush of foam and bubbles that often spray out of the top. As much as people like to drink fizzy bottles of champagne today, however, when French monks first invented the drink many centuries ago, these bubbles caused problems.

Champagne, like wine, is made from crushed grape juice that is stored in wooden barrels for many months. As the juice breaks down over time - a process called fermentation - its flavor becomes more concentrated, producing a sharp winy taste. Originally, this is as far as the fermentation process was typically taken. Traditional French champagne was originally a still, pinkish wine with a sharp, acidic taste.

In medieval times, however, wine growers in France began experimenting with the fermentation process by pouring the champagne wine into bottles, along with a mixture of other wine types, sugars, and yeast, all in an attempt to improve the wine's taste. Unfortunately, as this tended to happen around five or six months after the grape harvest, it often coincided with the warm spring and summer months in central France - and all that extra heat soon began to have an unwanted side effect!

As the temperatures in the French countryside began to rise, the yeast in the champagne bottles began to work overtime and began naturally producing a huge amount of carbon dioxide gas. The more gas the yeast produced, the more the pressure inside the bottles would grow until eventually the buildup would become too great and the bottle would either burst open, or explode altogether, throwing glass and the champagne all over the floor! As a result, the winemakers of the time began working on ways of limiting the gases and fizziness of the champagne, to stop it from blowing up its bottles - but across the English Channel in Britain, other people had a different idea.

Some winemakers began instead to develop stronger glass bottles, which could withstand the buildup of pressure inside the champagne. This kept the gas in the drink and in the bottle until it was time to open it and serve it. Champagne may have been invented in France, ultimately, but it was English bottle makers who developed the vessels strong enough to store it - and in doing so, kept its bubbles!

THE TRAGIC STORY
OF THE CPR DUMMY

If you have ever done a first aid course - which is an extremely useful thing to do! - Then you may have seen a model human face and chest which is used to teach so-called CPR breathing. CPR, or cardiopulmonary resuscitation, is a technique used to keep the heart and lungs of a patient who has stopped breathing for themselves going by hand. This is done by pressing down rhythmically on their chest and breathing air forcefully into their mouths.

Since the technique was first developed, it has become standard practice among first aid responders, doctors, and paramedics alike, and has saved countless lives the world over. But what about the doll on which this groundbreaking technique is practiced? Who can we credit with inventing that? Incredibly, the origins of the CPR doll date all the way back to the 1800s!

It was sometime in the 1880s that the body of a young woman was pulled from the River Seine in Paris. How the girl had died, who she was, and how old she was were all unknown, but the doctor who took care of her body after her death was so enamored of her beautiful face - and so determined to identify her - that he took a wax cast of her head.

As news of the tragic drowned girl spread across the city, many more casts of the doctor's mask were produced in an attempt to identify her. Before long, what had begun as a simple attempt to solve a mystery death had spawned a new trend. All fashionable houses in Paris had a model of the woman's face hung on their walls! Even famous writers like Albert Camus, the author of *The Three Musketeers*, wrote of her mask and her face in his work.

Sadly, the mystery was never solved, and the identity of the drowned woman has never been worked out. Around 80 years after her death, however, the fact that her face had become so famous led medical inventors Peter Safar and James Elam to use it as the basis of a dummy they had created on which to practice CPR breathing. Almost every CPR model still uses the girl's face to this day!

THE CHEF WHO MADE UP NACHOS ON THE SPUR OF THE MOMENT!

Some inventors give their names to their inventions. The diesel engine, for instance, is named after the German engineer Rudolph Diesel. The Colt handgun is named after its inventor Samuel Colt. And even the biro ballpoint pen is named after its Hungarian inventor, Laszlo Biro. But there is something very bizarre on this list of inventions named after their inventors: nachos.

According to legend, it was sometime in the mid-1940s that a man named Ignacio "Nacho" Anaya was working as the maître d' of a restaurant in the town of Piedras Negras, Mexico. One night, a group from the nearby border town of Eagle Pass, Texas, dropped in on Nacho's restaurant looking for something to eat. Having led them to a table, Nacho headed into the kitchen to see what the chef could rustle up for them - only to find that the chef was nowhere to be seen!

Faced with either turning the group away or else cooking for them himself, Nacho improvised with whatever he could lay his hands on in the restaurant's kitchen. He prepared a dish of tortilla chips topped with salsa, jalapenos, sour cream, grilled cheese, and anything else he could find! The made-up dish proved a hit with his customers, and before long, Ignacio's "Nachos" had become a permanent fixture on his restaurant's menu!

NOTES ABOUT POST ITS

In 1968, a scientist named Spencer Silver, who was working in the famous 3M laboratories, was given the task of coming up with a new super-strong adhesive. After several weeks' work, Silver had bizarrely managed to come up with the complete opposite: a very mild, weak adhesive that - although able to hold two things together - could easily be removed, without leaving any residue or stickiness behind. He noted that the "microspheres" of adhesive material he had produced were "strong enough to hold papers together, but weak enough to allow the papers to be pulled apart again without being torn." Silver presented his idea to several other 3M scientists, but thinking that his discovery had little real purpose, he shelved his research and carried on.

It was not until six years later, in 1974, that a fellow 3M scientist named Art Fry struck upon an idea. One evening while singing in a local choir, Fry decided that a bookmark he could use in his music book that would keep his page securely, without damaging the paper it was stuck to, would prove most useful. Immediately, he remembered the weak adhesive Silver had explained to him several years earlier, and on his return to the laboratories, the pair set about making a set of nonpermanent sticky bookmarks. As it happens, the paper tags they made had a lot more uses than just keeping a page - and before long, Post-It notes, as they became known, were being marketed as labels, name tags, notes, paper placeholders, and much, much more!

HOW SACCHARIN WAS INVENTED BY ACCIDENT

It is not just Corn Flakes and Post-It Notes that were invented by mistake - you can add the popular sweetener saccharin to that list as well!

Saccharin was the first commercially available artificial sugar-replacement sweetener the world had ever seen. It was invented way back in 1879, by a scientist named Constantin Fahlberg, who was working in the science laboratories of the famous Johns Hopkins University in Baltimore.

Fahlberg was actually working with a harmless chemical compound named benzoic sulfimide - a chemical that can be made from coal tar, a natural bitumen-like byproduct of coal and gas production. Then he happened to notice a sweet taste in his mouth. He rightly figured out that the sweet flavor must have come from the benzoic sulfimide and soon set about manufacturing the chemical in larger quantities to see if its sweetness had commercial applications.

Before long, saccharin, as Fahlberg named his discovery, had taken the nutritional world by storm as a cheap, low-calorie alternative to regular sugar. Championed by Theodore Roosevelt as an easy way to lower the sugar levels in your diet, and in doing so lose a little weight, saccharin proved even more popular during the world wars when sugar was in short supply around the world. It has remained popular ever since!

DID YOU KNOW?

○ Benjamin Franklin invented bifocal spectacles.

○ Pasteurization is the name of a process in which milk is heated to a specific temperature to make it safe to drink. It is named after a scientist called Louis Pasteur!

○ Thomas Edison proposed to his wife using Morse code.

○ In 1893, a woman named Margaret Wilcox filed a patent in the USA for a machine that could wash a person's clothes and kitchenware at the same time.

○ Bubble wrap packaging was invented by accident. The people who invented it were actually trying to invent three-dimensional wallpaper!

○ The Nobel Prizes are named after Alfred Nobel - who invented dynamite!

○ The Jacuzzi bathtub is named after the Jacuzzi brothers!

DISCOVERIES

DARWIN'S FINCHES AND THE DISCOVERY OF EVOLUTION

Today the English scientist Charles Darwin is known for coming up with the theory of evolution: the gradual development of a creature over time, through a process of natural selection. Darwin's theory, which is now widely accepted as scientifically true, is that tiny changes in a species over time gradually become permanent features if those changes improve on previous forms of the same animal. It is this theory that explains why some creatures develop extraordinary features and anatomies, like a giraffe's extra-long neck - which the species developed over time, longer and longer, to reach the tops of trees to feed where other animals could not.

But how did Darwin come up with such an extraordinary idea in the first place? Well, it was way back in the 1830s that Darwin traveled from England to the Galapagos Islands, a tiny group of islands off the west coast of South America, on board his scientific research vessel the *HMS Beagle*.

Arriving in the Galapagos Islands, Darwin noticed that there were around 20 different species of finches scattered across the islands, each of which seemed perfectly suited to its habitat and diet. One finch, known as the Galapagos ground finch, had a short, thick, stubby beak - the perfect beak for feeding on tough seeds on the ground. Another, the Galapagos warbler finch, had a much narrower and slenderer beak, which it used to pick out and feed on tiny insects hiding among the leaves in the trees. While another, known as the woodpecker finch, had a strong, pointed beak, which it used to pick up sticks to poke grubs out of holes in tree branches, like a fisherman.

These birds had developed in complete isolation, Darwin noted, and he began to imagine that they might all have shared a single common ancestor. Thousands of years ago, Darwin thought, a small population of just one species of bird must have arrived on the islands from the South American mainland. The birds began to breed, and over dozens and dozens of generations, developed a series of adaptations that allowed each one to take advantage of a single source of food. The basic notion of what Darwin would eventually call his theory of evolution had been put in place - thanks to some birds on the other side of the world!

RACE TO THE BOTTOM: HOW SCIENTISTS DISCOVERED THE COLDEST POSSIBLE TEMPERATURE

The coldest temperature that is possible to reach anywhere in the known universe is called "absolute zero." On the Celsius temperature scale, it is equal to –273.15 °C, or –459.67 °F on the Fahrenheit temperature scale. But how do we know that the universe cannot get any colder than this? And who first discovered this temperature in the first place?

It was back in the 1700s that scientists in Europe first began experimenting with, various gases - including air - and began attempting to reduce their temperatures as far as possible. Some scientists noticed that gases appeared to lose some of their mass and "contracted" as their temperatures were lowered. This discovery led to many scientists believing there must be a lower limit to this cooling process, at which point gases cannot contract anymore and so the temperature being impacted on them cannot go any further down. These early scientists called this theoretical freezing point the point of "infinite cold."

It was a century later, in the mid-1800s, that the English scientist William, Lord Kelvin, began investigating the notion of infinite cold himself. Based on his own observations of the behavior of gases and other material at low temperatures, he calculated that the lowest possible temperature must be around –273 °C. So confident was he that his workings were correct, that he introduced a new temperature scale using this low point as its basis. So, while the Celsius scale uses the freezing point of water as its 0° C point, on the so-called Kelvin temperature, 0° K is absolute zero—-273.15 °C (–459.67 °F)—with temperatures rising from there.

As technologies improved and ever more scientific research was conducted, Lord Kelvin's theories were eventually proved to be true, and since the 1950s, the Kelvin temperature scale, not Celsius or Fahrenheit, has been the standard temperature scale of many branches of science!

GALAXIES BEYOND GALAXIES:
THE DISCOVERIES OF EDWIN HUBBLE

So far in this book we have already met the American astronomer Edwin Hubble, who in the mid-1900s proved that the stars and galaxies outside of our own were moving away from ours, the Milky Way. His discovery proved that our entire universe is still expanding, and in doing so, all but proved that the Big Bang Theory is correct. But as well as providing the proof for our understanding of the origin of the universe, perhaps Hubble's greatest discovery was the fact that there are other galaxies beyond ours at all.

Before the 1900s, many scientists and astronomers believed that the Milky Way was so enormously vast that it must surely be the only galaxy in existence. In other words, the Milky Way - the galaxy in which Earth is located - must be the entire universe. Some of the other galaxies that astronomers had observed before then, like the famous Andromeda galaxy, were presumed by many people simply to lie on the very fringes of the Milky Way, and therefore, still part of our own galaxy. In 1923, however, Hubble turned the astronomical world on its head when he discovered that ours is not the only galaxy out there. He found that the outlying galaxies around our own, like Andromeda, are in fact far further away than we had ever imagined - and so must be considered galaxies in their own right.

THE LAB MISTAKE THAT GAVE US PENICILLIN

Penicillin is one of the world's most widely used and effective antibiotics. Used to treat bacterial infections the world over, it is one of modern medicine's truly great discoveries. But as useful as penicillin has proved to be, its discovery was actually a complete accident!

It is an early 20th-century Scottish chemist named Dr. Alexander Fleming who is credited with the discovery and eventual production of penicillin. In 1928, Fleming returned from a vacation to find that a glass dish containing a sample of a type of bacteria, called staphylococcus, had accidentally been left growing on the windowsill of his laboratory. When Fleming went to clean the dish out and sanitize it, he noted that a mold that had begun growing in the dish had apparently prevented the bacteria from growing. When he examined the mold sample under his microscope, Fleming noted that the mold apparently was able to produce some kind of chemical that acted as a self-defense mechanism, preventing the bacteria from affecting it and in turn holding the staphylococcus bacteria's growth back. He called the substance the mold produced "penicillin" and began writing up his findings.

Having completed his investigation of the mold, Fleming presented his new discovery to the scientific world later that year. To his surprise, many of his fellow scientists were not impressed by his discovery and failed to see the importance of it. Fleming spent several more years trying to make a commercially useful sample of penicillin with little progress, and by the 1930s, he was forced to end his research and shelved his work.

It was not until 1937 that another team of scientists, based at Oxford University, stumbled across Fleming's work, and began to develop a sample of penicillin themselves. Again, progress was painfully slow. The team found that they needed to produce gallons and gallons of mold-rich fluid - brewed up in a mixture of bathtubs, milk churns, and even hospital bed pans! - To extract only a few ounces of penicillin. But over time, their production techniques improved, and the team was able to extract ever larger quantities of penicillin from their work - yet still not enough to make the process worthwhile.

At long last, in 1941 one of the Oxford team traveled to the United States and there set up a second laboratory in which to work on the production and extraction of penicillin antibiotics. Working from a base in Peoria, Illinois, the team began looking for different strains of the original penicillin mold that might be able to produce richer quantities than the mold Fleming had originally discovered. Eventually, a mold growing on a rotting cantaloupe melon was found to produce six times the amount of penicillin that Fleming and the Oxford team had been able to extract. The production of workable antibiotics was suddenly made possible!

THAT TIME BENJAMIN FRANKLIN ELECTROCUTED A TURKEY..., AND HIMSELF!

As well as being an important statesman and one of America's Founding Fathers, Benjamin Franklin is also well known as a scientist responsible for some truly extraordinary inventions and discoveries. Many of his scientific endeavors involved his work with electricity, including the famous experiment in which he (supposedly!) flew a kite in a thunderstorm to prove that metals are useful electrical conductors. Not all of Franklin's experiments went quite well, however.

At Christmas 1750, for instance, Franklin used his interest in electricity to dream up a rather bizarre experiment. Wanting to kill a turkey to cook his family and friends for Christmas dinner, Franklin built up an electrical charge in two vast glass chambers and decided to electrocute the bird rather than kill it using more traditional techniques. Unfortunately, Franklin had not quite arranged the charge correctly, and as he approached the bird with the electrodes he hoped to use in the experiment, he took the entire electrical charge he had generated into his arms.

According to the bystanders, there was an enormous explosive bang and a huge flash of light, and Franklin - stunned senseless and knocked to the floor by the electric shock - was laid out cold on the floor. As he regained his consciousness, Franklin noted that his entire body continued to shake, and he had a painful tingling numbness in his arms for several days. Happily, he survived the accident, and the only permanent damage was to his pride!

JONATHAN SWIFT AND
THE MOONS OF MARS

Today, Jonathan Swift is perhaps best known as an author of the grand adventure story, *Gulliver's Travels*. His classic book tells the story of a man named Gulliver, who travels to several remarkable and weird and wonderful lands, encountering bizarre creatures, and wild races of both giants and tiny miniature people. And in one of the episodes in Swift's book, Gulliver travels to a vast floating island in the sky, named Laputa. There, he meets a society of very intelligent but small-minded people who know much of the world but have no interest or experience in using their knowledge practically.

Fascinated by science, mathematics, and astronomy, the people of Laputa have built a vast glass dome on their floating island, from which they examine the heavens, the stars, and planets. It is from here that they have noticed that the planet Mars, Swift wrote in his book, has two moons.

Swift published *Gulliver's Travels* almost 300 years ago, in 1726. It was, of course, an entirely fictional story. Yet, around 150 years after Swift made up this story of Laputa's astronomers and their fictional discovery of Mars' moons, in 1877, the American astronomer Asaph Hall made a rather unexpected discovery of his own: the planet Mars *did indeed have two moons!*

Just as Swift had predicted in his book more than a century earlier, Hall's observations of the Red Planet showed that it had two small natural satellites - the planet's only two moons - which he named Phobos and Deimos. Swift could have had no idea that Mars indeed had a pair of moons in its orbit, and his description of them in his book is, of course, just a coincidence - but it is nevertheless a very remarkable one!

HOW ISAAC NEWTON SPLIT LIGHT INTO THE SPECTRUM

When you look up to the sky on a rainy day, you might be lucky enough to see a rainbow arching its way from one side of the sky to the other. This band of colors - from red to violet - is formed by bright white light from the Sun being split apart into its different component lights. This produces a vast colored band we know now as the spectrum.

Aside from coming up with the theory behind the Earth's gravitational pull, Sir Isaac Newton can also be thanked for our understanding of the colors hidden inside pure white light. Newton had long been interested in the science of light, known as optics. In 1665, Newton noticed that when clear, bright sunlight shining through the window of his laboratory was focused on a glass prism (a three-dimensional triangular shape), the light exiting the prism on the other side was not white, but contained pure bands of color: red, orange, yellow, green, blue, indigo (pale purple), and violet (richer purple).

This experiment, Newton believed, showed that what we recognize as colors must all originate in pure, clear, white light. By demonstrating that white light can be split apart into its constituent colors, meanwhile, Newton paved the way for later scientists and physicists to continue his experiments. They proved that different colors are formed by beams of light having different wavelengths, which are picked up by special cells in our eyes and identified as distinct shades - precisely the kinds of colors you can see in a rainbow!

ARCHIMEDES' BATHTUB

One of the most famous experimental discoveries in the history of science belongs to an Ancient Greek scientist named Archimedes, who lived on the island of Sicily, in southern Italy, around 2,200 years ago, in the mid-3rd century BCE.

Archimedes was an astronomer, a mathematician, and a physicist, and he made several major steps forward in a number of different branches of sciences and mathematics. His reputation as a great scientific mind led to Archimedes becoming close to the king of Syracuse, Hieron II, who called on his skills one day after being brought a new crown. King Hieron had earlier given a block of gold to a local metal worker and asked him to make for him a new solid gold crown for him to wear in his palace. When the metal worker later returned with the new crown for the king, Hieron became suspicious and began to think that the metal worker had kept some of the gold for himself. Wanting to know the truth, King Hieron called upon Archimedes to find out a way to see if the metal worker had been honest or not, without destroying his work.

Archimedes struggled with the king's problem for several days, until one morning - when he stepped into his bathtub! As he lowered himself into the bath, Archimedes happened to notice that the level of the water in the tub rose. And what is more, the more of his body that Archimedes placed in the water, the higher the level went until, at last, he was entirely submerged below the surface and the displaced water was spilling over the edge of the tub. Archimedes had, he discovered, solved the king's problem and he leapt from his bathtub with a cry of "Eureka!" - the Greek word for "I have found it!"

Archimedes had discovered one of the foundational parts of what would become known as the Archimedes Principle: the amount of water displaced by something being lowered into it must be equal to the mass of the material itself. Or, as Archimedes actually stated in his work *On Floating Bodies*, "Any floating object displaces its own weight of fluid."

Archimedes could then return to King Hieron with a solution to his problem. Placing a block of gold, the same size as that which he gave to the metal worker, into a tub of water should displace precisely the same amount of liquid as placing the crown into a tub of water. If the crown displaced less water, the king could know for sure that the metal worker had kept some of the gold for himself!

DID YOU KNOW?

○ The C in Einstein's famous equation e = mc^2 stands for the speed of light - because the speed of light is a Constant!

○ The famous astronomer Galileo was able to discover so much of space because of improvements he made to his own telescope - which allowed him to see things 20 times clearer than anyone else!

○ The word "cell" was coined by a British biologist named Robert Hooke, who discovered that living things are made of "cells" way back in the 1600s.

○ Christopher Columbus wasn't the first person to discover the world was round. In fact, the Greek thinker Aristotle believed that the Earth was round more than 2,000 years ago!

○ The structure of DNA was discovered by scientists James Watson and Francis Crick in the 1950s. It stands for "deoxyribonucleic acid"!

○ The first person to prove that blood circulates around the body was the physician William Harvey nearly 400 years ago! He published his findings in 1628.

○ The ability to "loop" a computer program was discovered and developed by a female computer scientist called Ada Lovelace - way back in the 19th century!

NATURE

THE SHARK THAT LIVED FOR 500 YEARS

Human beings, even those who follow the best diets and strictest exercise regimes, typically tend to live no longer than 100 years old. Some so-called "super-centenarians" do sometimes live longer than that. The oldest person who ever lived was a French woman who died in 1997 at the age of 122! However, such long-lived people are very unusual.

Other animals, however, live much longer. There are reports that some large crocodiles have lived longer than 120 years; some giant tortoises have lived closer to 200 years old; and some sea creatures, like urchins and deep-sea clams, have been known to live even longer than that. One of the oldest creatures that has ever lived, however, is a peculiar species of fish called a Greenland shark.

Living deep in the Arctic waters around Greenland and the islands in the far north of Canada, very little is known about the life cycles of Greenland sharks. This is because their habitat is so beyond the reach of humanity. But in 2016, a study of the eye tissue taken from several sharks found out something truly remarkable about them.

Using the same technique - known as carbon dating - that is often used to analyze archeological specimens, the shark's eye tissue could be carbon-dated with remarkable accuracy. This allowed the scientists who conducted the study to age the sharks. Some of the sharks they looked at were found to be around 200–300 years old. One specimen may have been born as far back as the early 1500s and as such was likely over 500 years old! Greenland sharks are ultimately the longest-lived complex animals on the planet.

FEATHERED DINOSAURS?

Picture a dinosaur in your mind. You might imagine a huge scaly lizard-like animal, something rather like a gigantic crocodile. But recently, archeologists who study dinosaurs and their remains - known as paleontologists - have become increasingly convinced that dinosaurs were not covered in scales, but rather large barb-like feathers - a little like gigantic birds!

But how do we know that dinosaurs had feathers, when the very last of them died out in an enormous asteroid strike 65 million years ago?

In the mid-1990s, scientists announced the discovery of a new kind of dinosaur whose skeleton they had found in a remote region of China, which they called the *Sinosauropteryx* (a name meaning "Chinese winged lizard"). The creature's remains were almost entirely intact, so that the scientists who discovered it could tell that it was a new kind of two-legged dinosaur, which would have walked upright like a Tyrannosaurus Rex. As well as having all the usual features of a lizard-like dinosaur, however, the skeleton of the *Sinosauropteryx* was surrounded by the imprint of a fine network of barbs known as a "pelage." This strange envelope of lines, the scientists explained, was likely the remains of a covering of feathers. The lines surrounding the dinosaur's skeleton, ultimately, had been left by the tough central barbs or "filaments" of each of its individual plumes.

The discovery changed what we knew about dinosaurs almost overnight: some later species of dinosaurs, it now seemed likely, were indeed covered in thick early feathers, from which modern birds and their plumage would later have evolved.

Some questions remain, however. We do not know whether all later dinosaurs had similar plumage, for instance, and we do not know at what point during the hundreds of millions of years in which dinosaurs walked the earth that feathers first emerged. As ever more remains of apparently feathered dinosaurs are discovered, however, we will no doubt come to find out more about these peculiar ancient animals - and learn more about how they eventually evolved into everything from sparrows to chickens to ostriches!

THE BIRD THAT TAKES ON
THE WORLD'S LONGEST MIGRATION

Lots of different kinds of animals take part in a yearly migration, moving often vast distances across the face of Earth to find warmer or better grounds to feed, rear their young, or else see out the cold winter months. Some of the animal kingdom's longest migration journeys are taken on by large animals like caribou (or Arctic reindeer) and African wildebeest. But at the opposite end of the scale, some remarkably long and perilous journeys are taken on by some far smaller and much more surprising creatures.

Some North American monarch butterflies, for instance, flutter more than 3,000 miles each year from the borderlands of the southern provinces of Canada down to the southern United States, along the border with Mexico. Others complete an eastward journey that is almost as long, which takes them over the Appalachian Mountains.

Likewise, the bar-headed goose is an Asian species of water bird whose yearly migration takes them from their wintering grounds in central and southern India, northward into the middle of China to breed. In their way are the Himalayas Mountains - the highest mountains in the world - which the birds have to fly over in order to reach their destination. There are even reports from mountaineers and explorers who have apparently seen flocks of geese flying by while they are climbing up Mount Everest!

The world's longest migration of any animal, however, belongs to a very unassuming animal indeed. The tiny Arctic tern is a small seabird, only around 12 inches in length and weighing around four ounces. Despite its relatively small size, however, the birds complete a full circuit of Earth every year, traveling from the north pole to the south pole and back to breed. This single flight alone, from the Arctic to the Antarctic, is over 18,500 miles in length. Plus, when the seasons change and the northern hemisphere begins to warm and the southern hemisphere is plunged into the long, dark winter, the birds fly back again. That means they complete this immense journey twice every year!

THE WITCHES' WIND: ARGENTINA'S DISHEARTENING WEATHER PHENOMENON

Sometimes when it is cold and dark and rainy and gloomy outside, you might wake up in the morning and not feel your best. Compared to when the sun is shining and the birds are singing, a cold, wet, miserable day can make you feel just as miserable yourself! This is an example of something called *cyclonopathy* - the tendency of some people to feel a bit down and sometimes even a bit unwell during the approach of bad weather. But in one part of the world, this has become such a problem that the weather condition that causes it has become known as "the witches' wind!"

In the bottom-most regions of South America, the cold, wet, polar winds blowing in off the Pacific Ocean are forced up the high Andes Mountains that run along the border of Chile and Argentina. As this cold, wet air is forced upward, it produces huge rainstorms and snowstorms on both sides of the mountains, as well as covering the Andes mountaintops in a thick layer of snow. But having deposited all its water on the mountainsides, on the other side of the Andes, this wind warms and dries out as it falls down into the open plains of Argentina. As it does so, this hot, dry, wind, which is known locally as the *zonda* wind, can blow incredibly strongly, reaching gale force speeds over 100 mph!

But as well as carrying hot, dry air down the mountainside, the bizarre *zonda* weather system has another strange effect. The native tribes and other local people living on the Argentine grasslands often report feeling depressed when the zonda blows in! Their mood does not start to lift until the system has passed, typically 12 to 23 hours after it began. For that reason, as well as being known by the local Spanish name "zonda," the locals have named it the *huayrapuca*, or "witches' wind" - because their anxious, ill feeling seems almost to have been caused by witchcraft!

THE PITOHUI: THE WORLD'S ONLY POISONOUS BIRD

Have you heard of a bird called the "pitohui"? There is probably a good reason why if you have not, as this family of around ten relatively small thrush-like birds are found only in the rainforests of the island of New Guinea, north of Australia. But there is a reason why you might want to stay away from the pitohui - it is the only poisonous species of bird in the entire world!

Bizarrely, some species of pitohui - the hooded pitohui and the variable pitohui - have a powerful toxin in their skin and feathers. It is similar to the toxic chemicals produced by the skin of some amphibians, like the poison arrow frogs found in the Amazon rainforest. Quite why the birds are able to produce these chemicals is unclear. This has puzzled scientists and animal experts ever since the bird was first discovered.

One theory is that the birds use these toxins to prevent themselves from catching ticks and other parasites, which might otherwise bite their skin and feed on their blood. Another claims that the birds produce the toxins to ward off potential predators, like snakes, cats, humans, and other larger birds, like hawks and owls.

As for how the birds can produce the chemical at all, that is thought to be an easier question to answer! The birds routinely feed on a special kind of beetle known as a choresine beetle, which in turn contains powerful toxins in its body. The birds seem to be unaffected by these chemicals. Instead, they take advantage of these toxins to make themselves poisonous and protect themselves in turn!

CARLOS JARED
AND THE VENOMOUS FROGS
OF THE AMAZON

Speaking of toxic animals, let's return to those toxic frogs of the Amazon rainforest. You might have heard tales before of frogs and toads that can produce oily toxins through their skin, rather like human beings can produce sweat through our skin. But in 2016, a Brazilian animal expert and scientist named Carlos Jared discovered that one particular species of frog native to South America has a very different defense mechanism, which it uses in a quite remarkable way!

Jared's research involved describing and investigating the behavior of a species of frog known as Greening's tree frog. From the outside, the frog looks rather like any other: it has large black and yellow eyes, damp green skin, and a broad mouth. It also has wide feet and toes that it uses to clamber around the rocks and vegetation of the plains and cactus forests of northeastern Brazil. But one day, when Jared was handling one of the frog specimens he had caught to investigate, the frog jerked its head forward and "head-butted" Jared's hand. At first, he thought nothing of it, but within a matter of minutes Jared's entire arm had begun to throb painfully, and the intense pain went on to last for around the next five hours!

What Jared had discovered, quite by accident, is that Greening's tree frog has a bony structure inside its head, which is covered in a series of short spines or barbs that partly protrude through the skin of the frog's face. When threatened, the frog thrusts its head forward, piercing the skin of any potential predator or attacker. It then uses these sharp spiny projections in its face to inject a toxin into the attacker's body - just like a doctor injecting medicine into a patient! Plus, Greening's tree frog turned out to be just one of a handful of other similar species of so-called "casque" frogs found in northern Brazil.

This amazing discovery meant that although many other frog species are able to produce toxins and poisons that can harm or even kill their predators, the casque frogs of South America are the only species that are capable of forcefully injecting their poison directly into their intended target!

HOW OWLS FLY SO QUIETLY

If you have ever been lucky enough to spot an owl while on a walk through the woods, then you might have noticed just how perfectly adapted to their surroundings and their hunting technique the birds are. For one thing, owls have exceptionally long curled claws, known as talons, which allow them to grasp onto their prey very tightly - often killing it instantly. Their large round eyes, coupled with their ability to rotate their heads almost 180 degrees in both directions, give them excellent vision. And the birds' round faces deflect any incoming sounds - like the quiet squeaking of a mouse - directly into their ears, giving them pinpoint-accurate hearing too.

But although owls are capable of hearing even the slightest sound made by their prospective prey, how do they remain so quiet when it comes to tracking their prey down? Or, in other words, while the owl can hear the mouse squeaking, what stops the mouse from hearing the owl flying in to snatch it up for its dinner?!

For one thing, owl's flight feathers are far softer than many other birds' flight feathers, giving them a texture similar to velvet. This softness helps the deaden the sound of the bird's wingbeats, just like thick velvet curtains might help to deaden the sound coming from outside in a room.

Not only that, however, but an owl's wing feathers have a slightly bumpy or "serrated" edge, not a smooth edge, which helps to break up and deflect the turbulent air passing over and under the wing as the bird flies. So rather than noisily flapping their way through the air like another bird might, the owl's feathers help to break up the air into dozens of smaller, quieter air channels known as "microturbulences." This allows them to pass through the air almost completely silently!

THE LAST THYLACINE

Have you ever heard of an animal called an "endling"?

Well, an endling is not actually a specific type of animal at all - instead, it is the final surviving individual animal of a particular species. So, when the endling dies at the end of its life, the entire species it represents tragically dies with it. And one of the most famous endlings in all of natural history is the very last thylacine.

Also known as a Tasmanian tiger, the thylacine was a large dog-like mammal, with a broad mouth - containing 46 teeth and pale brown and black striped fur. A member of the marsupial family of animals (alongside the likes of kangaroos and wallabies), the thylacine had a pouch on its belly in which its young would stay while they were being reared.

At one time, the animal was fairly widely spread across much of Australasia. Thylacine skeletons have been discovered everywhere from southern Australia to the islands of New Guinea and Indonesia in Southeast Asia. Over time, however, the animal's range decreased. By the turn of the last century, the only remaining wild thylacines lived in very remote parts of the island of Tasmania, off Australia's far southern coast.

Unfortunately, thylacines were such good hunters that they were seen as causing a threat to farmers' livestock. By the early 1900s, they had hunted almost into extinction. The very last individual thylacine - an unnamed female thylacine, which had been caught in a snare trap and handed over the Tasmania's Hobart Zoo - died in captivity in 1936. Although there are rumors that the creature may have survived in very remote locations in the wild, there has been no confirmed sighting of a wild thylacine ever since, meaning this final Hobart thylacine was tragically the species endling.

DID YOU KNOW?

○ A group of rhinoceroses is called a "crash."

○ Only two types of mammals lay eggs: platypuses and echidnas.

○ Hummingbirds are the only birds in the world that can fly backward.

○ A mole eats half its body weight in worms and insects every day!

○ The world's oldest tree is over 4,800 years old!

○ A polar bear's fur isn't white - if you were to look at one of its hairs closely, you would see that they are actually translucent.

○ Flamingos are the only animals that turn their heads upside to feed.

MYSTERIES

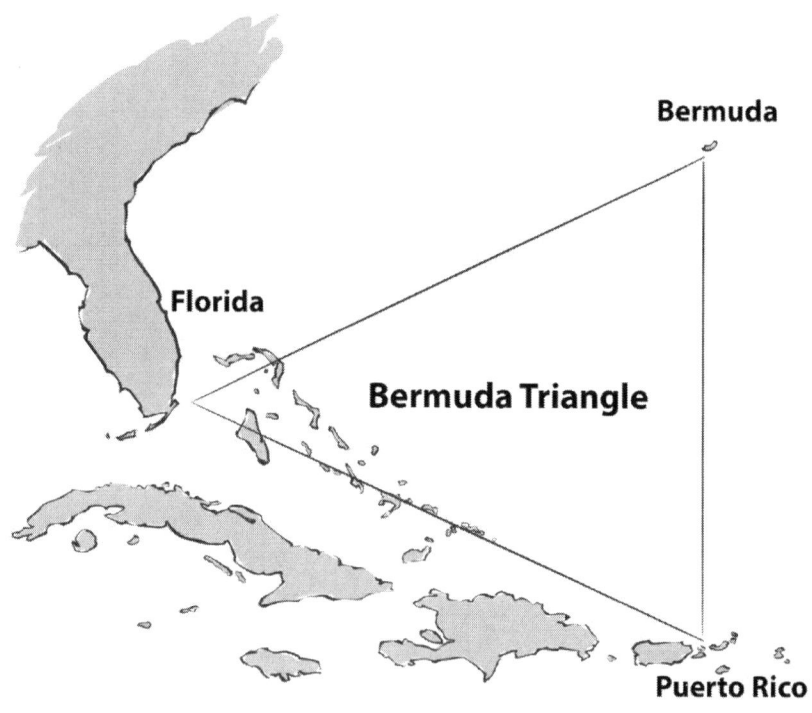

THE CURSE OF KING TUT'S TOMB

When the famous Egyptian pharaoh King Tutankhamun died, around 1324 BCE, he was placed inside a tomb that, over the centuries that followed, was gradually lost to the shifting sands of the eastern Sahara Desert. The tomb was not discovered again until 1922, when a British archeologist named Howard Carter used a mixture of local knowledge, historical research, and sheer luck to relocate Tutankhamun's tomb and reopen it for the first time in nearly 3,000 years.

King Tut's tomb turned out to be one of the largest, most well-stocked, and best-preserved of all the tombs in Egypt's famous Valley of the Kings. Unlike many of those around it, it had lain undisturbed for centuries and so had never been looted by burglars and graverobbers. The exquisite treasures Tutankhamun had been buried with were all still in place, just as they had been when the tomb was sealed. Understandably, the discovery caused a revelation in the early 1900s. After Carter had emptied and cataloged all of the tomb's contents, he put it on display in museums and galleries all around the world, with audiences queuing up around the blocks to get in and see the priceless artifacts he had found.

In the aftermath of the discovery, however, rumors of a curse began to appear. Some people were wary of the tomb's contents. They believed that bad luck would surely follow anyone who was involved in the tomb's discovery and the disturbance of the ancient king's belongings. Sure enough, just a few months after the tomb was uncovered, the wealthy financial backer of Carter's expedition, Lord Carnarvon, died suddenly in Egypt of an infected mosquito bite. In 1923, a wealthy American businessman named George Jay

Gould traveled to Egypt and visited the tomb. Yet before he had a chance to return home to the United States, he died suddenly of a fever in the south of France. In 1928, Arthur Mace - one of the excavators who had opened the tomb - died suddenly of a lung disease. And as the years ticked by, ever more names began to be added to the supposed list of victims of King Tut's curse, until at last, Howard Carter himself died in London, at the age of 64, in 1939.

As popular a story as the curse of King Tut has become, however, today most people dismiss it as nothing more than superstitious nonsense. The fact that the "curse" took a full 17 years to track down and kill the archeologist whose work had led to the tomb being opened seems to suggest that there was nothing supernatural going on here at all! But there are nevertheless many people who indeed believe that the tombs of Ancient Egypt were meant to be kept shut, and opening them and sharing their contents around the world is destined to bring all those involved bad luck...

THE BERMUDA TRIANGLE

The isolated island of Bermuda lies in the northern Atlantic Ocean, around 600 miles off the eastern coast of the United States. If you were to draw a line south from Bermuda, you would eventually reach the Caribbean island of Puerto Rico. From there, you could draw a line westward, connecting it to the state of Florida, and from Florida draw a line diagonally northeastward back up to Bermuda. Those three lines would ultimately form a triangle, covering a vast empty area of the open Atlantic Ocean that has become known as the "Bermuda Triangle."

For decades, the Bermuda Triangle has been known as the site of countless mysterious disappearances of ships, boats, airplanes, and other vessels and aircraft that have apparently ventured into this vast area of open sea and never been seen or heard from again. Rumors that something peculiar was happening in this area of the ocean first emerged in the 1940s and 50s, when the area became notorious among World War II pilots and aircraftmen. One of the very first Bermuda mysteries was reported in 1945, when a group of no less than five US Navy torpedo bomber aircraft flew into the Bermuda Triangle on a training mission, and all promptly disappeared.

As the years went by, ever more tales of disappearances like this one were recorded - and ever more wild theories explaining the disappearances began to be concocted. Some people claimed immense sea swells and waves were the problem, and that the ocean currents here grew so massive that the waves could swamp boats and knock planes from the sky. Others argued enormous waterspouts - tornado-like storms that form over the ocean - were to blame. Others thought storms, winds, and even glare from the

Sun were more likely. And then there were the people who believed the entire mystery to be the work of aliens and UFOs...

To this day, however, the mystery of what happens in the Bermuda Triangle - and quite why so many ships and aircraft have been lost inside it - remains unsolved.

THE CRIMES OF JACK THE RIPPER

Way back in 1888, Victorian London was gripped by a series of grisly murders committed by an unknown killer who became known as "Jack the Ripper."

The Ripper's five victims: Mary Ann Nichols, Annie Chapman, Elizabeth Stride, Catherine Eddowes, and Mary Jane Kelly - were all found killed in various locations across the Whitechapel area of central London. The brutal and bloody scenes of their murders showed that the Ripper was a horrifically violent and deranged killer, and as a result, the entire city was terrified of who and where he might strike next. As it happened, however, Jack the Ripper's crimes stopped almost as quickly as they had begun - the first murder was reported on August 31, and the last on November 9 - after which the Ripper seemingly never killed again.

Incredibly, despite becoming the talk of the entire city of London over the autumn of 1888, the Jack the Ripper murders have remained unsolved to this day. No one knows the identity of the murderer (or murderers!), the relationship of the killer to the victims, and why the killing stopped when they did. Several theories have been proposed over the days, and several high-profile figures from Victorian England have been put forward as potential Ripper suspects. These include a famous artist named Walter Sickert, the physician to the royal family, Sir William Gull, and even Queen Victoria's own grandson, Prince Albert Victor. Whether these, or any of the other proposed names, were indeed responsible for the killings has never been proved...

WHAT IS STONEHENGE FOR?

In the far southwest corner of England stands the ancient stone circle of Stonehenge. One of the most famous and popular monuments in all the British Isles, Stonehenge attracts tourists and visitors from all around the world, who like to wander among these ancient standing stones. They particularly like to do this at the changing of the seasons when it is presumed these stones would once have been the site of ancient rituals and performances.

Historians believe that ceremonies like those honoring the changing of the seasons have been carried out at the site of Stonehenge, known as Salisbury Plain, for around 10,000 years. The monument itself was built sometime later, probably around 3,000 to 5,000 years ago, between 3000 and 1500 BCE. Some of the graves and remains dug up around the site suggest that the people who came to Stonehenge might have traveled from as far away as the Mediterranean. Yet quite what brought them to England, and what Stonehenge was actually built for in the first place, remain complete mysteries!

Some people believe it might once have been a temple, or some early kind of church, used by the ancient Druids who once lived in Britain. Others claim it might have been used as a kind of sundial or giant timepiece, or even as a way of mapping the stars and keeping track of the movements of constellations. Another theory suggests it was perhaps used to play some kind of ancient game or sport. But then again, it may just have been a meeting place - a grand monument where important chieftains and tribal leaders might have known to come together to discuss the issues of the time. Unfortunately, the origins of Stonehenge have long since been forgotten, and as a result, its true purpose will likely never be known again.

THE LOCH NESS MONSTER

Is there a giant monster lurking beneath the waters of Loch Ness? If there were, there would certainly be enough room for it, as this one loch alone is so deep and so vast that it contains more water than all the lakes in England and Wales put together!

Tales of a giant creature living in Loch Ness date back to medieval times, when it was reported by the ancient British saint Columba that a monstrous water-dwelling animal had emerged from the water and bit a person swimming in the loch, before Columba commanded it back beneath the waves. The creature remained largely unseen and unreported until the 1900s, when a series of fresh reports of something lurking in the loch began to reemerge. Most claimed that the animal was a long-necked, dinosaur-like creature with a small head and flippers. This added fuel to the idea that an ancient plesiosaur - a kind of aquatic reptile that lived at the same time as the Jurassic dinosaurs - had perhaps become trapped in the lake and survived the extinction event that had wiped out all the others.

Unfortunately, evidence that such a creature could exist - or that the loch could support a population of such creatures - is lacking. Many people believe the tales to be nothing but local legends. Nevertheless, sightings of something unusual lurking beneath the loch's waters continue to make headlines today...

THE DISAPPEARANCE OF THE *MARY CELESTE*

The *Mary Celeste* was an American brigantine - a large two-masted sailing ship - that was built and launched from a port in Nova Scotia way back in 1861. Originally known as the *Amazon*, the ship was sold to America after being partly run aground and damaged in 1867 and relaunched as the *Mary Celeste* the following year.

After extensive renovations, the ship fell into use as a cargo vessel and in 1872 set sail from New York heading out across the Atlantic to Genoa, a port city in Italy. On board were hundreds of barrels of liquor, due to be sold on in port, as well as ten passengers and crew. Just over three weeks into the voyage, the ship stuck rough seas and harsh weather. On November 25, the ship's captain noted in its logbook that the vessel had come to within six nautical miles of the Azores, a small group of rocky volcanic islands off the coast of Africa. Ten days later, the crew of a British ship in the sea area of the Atlantic found the *Mary Celeste* sailing aimlessly in the open waters of the Azores. When the crew boarded the vessel to investigate, they found the entire ship abandoned. The cargo and all the passengers' and crew's belongings remained on board, with no sign or explanation of where or why they had left the ship. They had all, it seemed, simply vanished.

The fate of the *Mary Celeste* and its ten passengers persists as one of the most peculiar and unusual mysteries of the high seas in history and remains unsolved to this day.

AMELIA EARHART'S LAST FLIGHT

Amelia Earhart was perhaps the greatest female pilot of the early 20th century. Born in Kansas in 1897, Earhart originally worked in nursing during World War I and seemed destined to continue her career in medicine when a chance meeting with a Flying Ace fighter pilot led to her pursuing a career as a pilot instead. She took her first flying lesson in 1920, and before long had become an accomplished aviator with countless hours of experience. Gradually growing in fame and celebrity for her daredevil flights, Earhart made headlines all around the world in 1932 when she became the first woman in history to fly singlehandedly across the Atlantic Ocean.

Over the years that followed her transatlantic flight, Earhart continued to break records and establish aviation firsts. As a result, she was at the very height of her fame when, in 1937, she and her navigator Fred Noonan embarked on their most daring escapade yet. Together, they planned to fly around the world, giving Earhart the title of the first woman in aviation history to circumnavigate the globe.

Setting off from Oakland, California, on May 20, Earhart and Noonan's route took them across the mainland United States to the Caribbean, down to South America, and across the Atlantic to Africa, arriving in Senegal on June 8. From there, they continued the flight east, stopping in Sudan, India, Thailand, and Burma, before arriving in Darwin, in northern Australia, on June 28. The next leg of their flight was due to take them from Lae, a town on the east coast of New Guinea, to Howland Island, an uninhabited island in the Pacific Ocean. There, Earhart was due to meet with a

US supply ship. Somewhere between Lae and Howland Island, however, Earhart's plane disappeared.

Quite what happened to Earhart and Noonan on their record-setting flight is unclear. The leg between Lae and Howland Island was the longest of their flight, and at 20 hours in duration, was almost at the limit of what her aircraft could manage in a single flight. Some people believe the pair perhaps overshot the island, missing it due to low cloud cover, or else became disoriented when their navigation equipment failed and ended up running out of fuel and crashing into the ocean. Others claim the pair landed safely, but on another uninhabited island in the same region. Having used all their fuel to get there, and having missed their connecting supply ship, the pair would have been all but impossible to rescue. They would have been forced to live out their days alone on a desert island. Quite what happened to one of the most famous women in the world almost a century ago, therefore, remains a complete mystery.

THE ROANOKE DISAPPEARANCES

One of the longest-standing mysteries in American history is that of Roanoke Colony, a tiny colony of settlers that was established on a small island off the east coast of North America way back in 1587. Given the date of the colony's founding, Roanoke would be the oldest permanent colonial settlement in the United States today - if it had not been mysteriously abandoned just three years later.

The first few months in Roanoke after the arrival of the colonists in 1587 were tough. Food and fresh water were scarce, medical equipment was in short supply, and several of the early settlers fell ill. With little other option, the mayor of Roanoke, John White, set sail heading back to England in the hopes of returning with more supplies as quickly as he could. However, when he arrived back on the island in 1590, he found it completely abandoned.

Quite what happened to the colonists in that time is a complete mystery. Some outlandish theories claim that the settlers fell victim to witchcraft or sorcery, were driven mad with black magic, or else were savaged by some unknown monster lurking in the surrounding hills or waters. A more likely theory, however, is that the remaining settlers were unable to support themselves with what little supplies and local knowledge they had at their disposal. So, they simply joined forces with the local native Hatteras tribe and lived with them for the remainder of their time in the Americas. With little other than a handful of mysterious tree carvings to go on, however, it seems the true fate of the Roanoke colonists will forever be a mystery.

DID YOU KNOW?

○ Stonehenge is made of more than 90 individual stones...

○ ...though some historians think there might once have been more than 150!

○ The average weight of the stones at Stonehenge is 25 tons - but the heaviest, known as the Heel Stone, weighs more than 30!

○ The Roanoke territory was the brainchild of the English explorer Sir Walter Raleigh...

○ ...whose explorations in the New World were so successful that Elizabeth I knighted him for it!

○ Another of Amelia Earhart's firsts was that she was the first woman in the world ever to fly an autogiro - a kind of light aircraft, similar to an early helicopter!

○ Some people believe Jack the Ripper killed more people than we think he did - and in fact, six more murders from around the same time have since been linked to his case.

KINGS QUEENS

THE TIME HENRY VIII WRESTLED AGAINST THE KING OF FRANCE

Surely one of the most famous kings in all history has to be the English King Henry VIII. Known for his six wives (and their unpleasant fates), as well as establishing the Anglican church and fathering no less than three other English monarchs, Henry VIII certainly lived an interesting life. One of the more peculiar stories about Henry VIII is that, in his youth, he once challenged the King of France to a wrestling match - and, what is more, the young King Henry lost!

If you have seen pictures of Henry VIII before, you might be familiar with a king who was rather large and out of physical shape. That, however, was at the end of his life. In his youth, King Henry was actually surprisingly athletic and was known to be a strong, tall, strapping young man. He was also incredibly competitive - and in 1520, that brought him up against his physical match, the young French King, Francis I.

The venue was the so-called Field of the Cloth of Gold, a vast exposition - almost like a Tudor period World's Fair -that brought together the people and royal families of England and France in a grand open-air festival. Held in Calais, on the north coast of France, the Cloth of Gold festival featured music, archery, jousting, hunting, and all kinds of other sports and pursuits, all watched over by the two kings. And as the contest wore on, Henry came up with the idea that the two kings themselves should get in on all the fun.

Like Henry, King Francis was young and athletic, and so Henry challenged him to a wrestling bout in a simple feat of strength. Although Henry, who was 28 at the time, apparently fancied his chances against his counterpart, who was 25, it was Francis who took victory. According to onlookers, he attacked Henry at the hips and toppled him over, taking victory in the bizarre royal rumble in a matter of moments!

THE MADNESS OF
KING GEORGE

Another English king you might have heard tales of before is King George III, who ruled for a record-setting 59 years and 96 days, from 1760 until 1820. He remains England's longest-ruling king, and the third longest reigning monarch (after Queen Victoria and Elizabeth II). But as long as George's reign was, it was also somewhat disastrous. George III is famously the English king who oversaw the independence of America, and the loss of England's colonies - while the king himself is popularly said to have been completely mad.

Although tales of "the mad king" George III have been somewhat exaggerated over the years, records from his lifetime show that his behavior as king was rather bizarre. According to reports, the king would often begin talking wildly - using ever longer words and ever more overblown language - and often repeating himself, talking in circles, and making no sense whatsoever. He would forget to take breaths and talk for so long and so quickly that foam and spit would build up around his mouth. When his fits of wild madness became particularly bad, in fact, his pages and attendants would have to move the furniture away from him and have him sit or lie down on the floor, pinning him down in case he hurt himself.

Quite what caused the king's madness is unclear. Some historians have claimed that he perhaps suffered from bouts of the mental condition we now know as manic depression, or bipolar disorder, which can cause wild highs and depressive slumps. Others have suggested that his madness might have been caused by a dietary upset, or perhaps an internal infection for which he was not receiving the best treatment. No matter what was the cause of the king's extraordinary mood swings and madcap outbursts, however, at least some of the stories behind "The Mad King" label are, it seems, entirely true!

THE KING WHO THOUGHT HE WAS MADE OF GLASS

It was not just England who had a mad king, however. Across the English Channel in France, Charles VI of France had fallen into such a wild madness that he had become completely convinced that his entire body was made of glass!

Charles ruled over France for over 40 years, from 1380 until 1422. At first, he had proved a highly capable leader and led his armies into battle on several occasions across medieval Europe. In 1392, however, the king fell into madness on the battlefield and became so confused and deranged that he ended up attacking his own soldiers. After that, his madness slowly worsened, and the king was never the same again.

King Charles' mental state reached its peak in the early 1400s, when he began to experience wild delusions that he was made out of solid glass. As a result, he became terrified of moving his body too quickly, out of fear that his glass bones and body would shatter into pieces, killing him instantly. To avoid any such accidents, the king would reportedly remain completely stationary for long periods of time sitting on his throne. Later, he even had iron rods sewn into his clothes to keep his arms and legs completely straight for fear of bending them and shattering himself to pieces!

THE PRINCES IN THE TOWER

One of the eeriest tales in royal history is that of the two so-called Princes in the Tower - the young English King Edward V, and his brother Prince Richard, the Duke of York.

The two young brothers were the heirs to the English throne of medieval king Edward IV. On his death in 1483, the elder brother, the young Prince Edward - who was just 12 years old at the time - rose to succeed his father and was crowned King Edward V of England.

If anything were then to happen to him, his younger brother Richard would take the throne in his place. Now second in line to the throne behind Richard was the brothers' uncle, Richard, the Duke of Gloucester. And, according to royal legend, Duke Richard wanted the throne for himself - and was willing to stop at nothing to ensure he got it.

Given that Edward V was so young, for a time early on in his reign his uncle, Richard, stepped in as a caretaker king, making royal decisions and arrangements until he was old enough and wise enough to do so on his own. While preparations were being conducted for Edward's coronation ceremony, however, Richard sent him and his brother off to the Tower of London. The pair were never seen or heard from again, and in their absence, their uncle was free to claim the throne as his own as King Richard III.

Quite what happened to the young princes is unknown, but many people believe that King Richard had the pair imprisoned - or worse still, murdered - so he could take the throne for his own.

HENRY III'S *WHITE SHIP* DISASTER

Another peculiar and disastrous event in the history of the English royal family took place in 1120, during a trip to France under the reign of the medieval king Henry I.

King Henry had just one legitimate male heir to succeed him on his death, who was known as William, the Duke of Normandy. On the night of November 25, 1120, William - along with his father, the king, as well as dozens of members of their extended family and royal court - were all due to board a vessel called the *White Ship* to return to England following a short visit to the king's lands in northern France. At the last moment, however, King Henry was delayed, and so arrangements were made for him to travel back to England at a later time, while William and the remainder of the royal entourage were to continue on as planned.

The delay to the king's journey, however, had led to the passengers of the *White Ship* making the most of their free time by eating, drinking, and partying on board the ship. So, by the time the ship came to depart, many of the passengers - and many of its crew - were drunk and somewhat worse for wear! Shortly after leaving port in rough seas and in the dark winter night, ultimately, the ship soon came into trouble and ran aground on low-lying rocks off the French coast. It quickly began to take on water, and in the panic, the passengers began jumping overboard into the rough and icy seas, attempting to swim back to port. Tragically, despite there being perhaps as many as 300 people on board the *White Ship*, just one person survived.

The *White Ship* disaster effectively wiped out King Henry's entire family and line of succession. With all obvious heirs to the throne now dead, the event threw medieval England into a brief period of uncertainty and conflict that would become known as "The Anarchy."

MARIA ELEONORA, THE MADCAP QUEEN OF SWEDEN

England is not the only country to have such a bizarre royal past. Queen Maria Eleonora was a German princess who married into the Swedish royal family in the 17th century and ruled as Queen of Sweden, as the wife of Sweden's King Gustav II Adolph, from 1620 until 1632.

Queen Maria's time on the throne was not a happy one. Her husband was almost constantly away fighting wars on the European mainland, leaving her alone in a nation where she did not feel at home. In an attempt to secure a male heir to the throne, the couple had four children. Yet, three died, while the fourth - the only one to survive into adulthood - was a girl, and so could not carry on the king's line according to the monarchy's rules at the time. By now drifting into grief and madness, Queen Maria all but abandoned her only daughter. When news reached her that her husband, King Gustav, had been killed in battle, her mind was finally lost.

Driven mad with grief, when the king's body was returned to Sweden, Queen Maria had it kept in the royal bedroom so that she could still see and sleep beside her husband every day. When at long last she agreed to have her husband's body buried, she demanded his heart be removed from his body and placed in a solid gold casket so that she could keep it with her at all times. She never recovered from her husband's loss, and as her daughter took to the throne in his place, Queen Maria reportedly spent the remainder of her life weeping and crying constantly, often for days on end, alone in her room.

MUSTAFA I,
THE SULTAN WHO LIVED IN
A CAGE TWICE!

The Ottoman Empire was a vast and powerful collection of states that once covered a huge swath of Eastern Europe, Asia, North Africa, and the Middle East. Ruled over by a sultan, the throne of the Ottoman Empire was fiercely contested, and bitter disagreements often divided high-ranking Ottoman families as siblings and relationships clashed over their right to the sultan's throne. Often, in fact, some sultans would have their siblings, or their closest relatives, killed or exiled to remove the threat to their reign. One 17th-century sultan, Ahmet, could not bring himself to have his brother Mustafa killed, and instead had him imprisoned in a tiny cage in the palace.

That might have been the end of Mustafa's tale were it not for the fact that his elder brother, Sultan Ahmet, died suddenly in 1617 at the age of just 27. His court knew that they needed to elect a successor quickly, for fear that a usurper would claim the throne as his own. As a result, they had Mustafa removed from his cage after 14 years imprisonment and installed him as sultan instead.

Mustafa's isolated life, however, had taken its toll on his mind, and he proved an unsuitable leader. He was not smart or experienced enough to rule the empire alone. Although guided partly by his mother, Mustafa's rule was disastrous, and his court soon began to regret installing him as sultan. Eventually, the situation proved so unfavorable that Mustafa was overthrown, imprisoned once again in the palace, and a new sultan, Osman II, was installed in his place.

Fate had other things in store, however, and four years later in 1622, Osman II was assassinated. The sultan's court was left with little option but to reinstate Mustafa I as sultan once again! This second reign was very short-lived, however, and Mustafa was once again removed from power barely a year later. So, this extraordinary sultan ended up ruling one of the world's most powerful empires not once but twice - and in between, was kept in a cage inside the very palace from which he had reigned!

QUEEN VICTORIA, THE GRANDMOTHER OF EUROPE

Queen Victoria ruled over Great Britain for over 63 years, from 1837 until her death in 1901. In her extraordinarily long reign, she and her husband, Prince Albert, had nine children - Victoria, Edward, Alice, Alfred, Helena, Louise, Arthur, Leopold, and Beatrice. Almost all of them went on to marry into several of the other royal families of Europe, earning Queen Victoria the nickname of "The Grandmother of Europe."

Princess Victoria, for instance, married the future Emperor of Germany, Prince Frederick. Alfred married the Grand Duchess of Russia. Edward married the crown princess of Denmark. Arthur married Princess Louise of Prussia. Each of Queen Victoria's children in turn had children of their own. In total, Queen Victoria had no less than 42 grandchildren (and 87 great-grandchildren).

But as all of her children had married into other royal houses, Queen Victoria's bloodline - and therefore, that of the English royal family - is now connected to almost all of Europe's royal families. In fact, by the time of World War I, her grandchildren occupied the thrones of both Germany and the United Kingdom, despite the two nations being opponents!

DID YOU KNOW?

○ The only English king to be executed was King Charles I in 1649

○ Queen Elizabeth II spoke fluent French...

○ ...and was a fully trained mechanic!

○ William the Conqueror was crowned on Christmas Day.

○ Victoria and Queensland, Australia; Victoria in Canada; and the famous Victoria Falls in Africa are all named after Queen Victoria.

○ Only two of Henry VIII's wives outlived him - his final wife, Catherine Parr, and his fourth wife, Anne of Cleves...

○ ...who was also the longest-lived of all six of his wives!

SPORTS GAMES

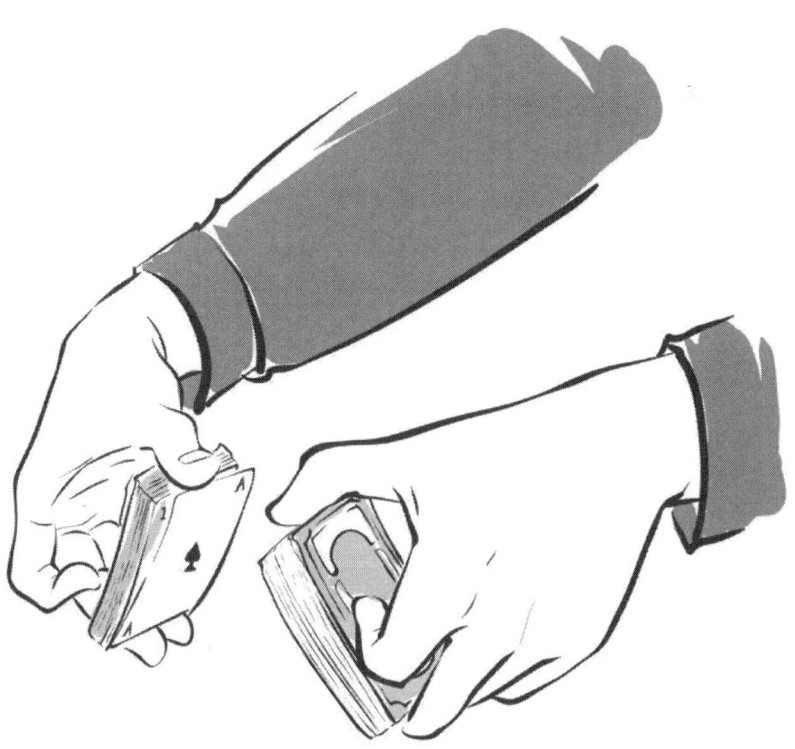

JESSE OWENS' RECORD BREAKING 45 MINUTES

American athlete Jesse Owens was one of the greatest sportsmen of the 20th century. A star of track and field, he won a record four gold medals at the 1936 Olympic Games in Berlin, Germany - famously taking the opportunity to protest against Germany's then-leader, Adolf Hitler, in the process!

Winning four gold medals in a single Olympics was an extraordinary feat (only one, Carl Lewis, has equaled Owens' achievement since!). Yet what makes Owens' medal haul even more impressive is that he won all four of his golds in the space of just *45 minutes!*

Owens' record-breaking day began at around 3:15 p.m. on May 25, when he took his first gold in the 100-yard dash (the precursor to the modern 100-meter sprint). In doing so, he equaled the current world record time of 9.4 seconds. Just ten minutes later, at 3:25 p.m., Owens moved from the track to set a new world record in the long jump, when he took gold with a leap of 8.13 m - the first eight-meter long jump scored in Olympic history!

Then, less than ten minutes after that at 3:34 p.m., Owens returned to the track for the 220-yard dash (equivalent to the modern 200 meters), taking gold and setting another world record with a finishing time of 20.3 seconds. Then finally, at 4:00 p.m., Owens lined up once more to take on the 220-yard hurdles race; once again, he finished first, taking the gold, and setting a new world record time of 22.6 seconds. Incredible!

WHEN THE OLYMPIC GAMES BECAME CRAFTY!

The Olympic Games are, of course, a sports competition, but precisely what sports are contested at the Olympics has changed over the years. In recent decades, modern events like BMX cycling have been added to the Olympic list of sports. In the earlier years, more old-fashioned sports like rope climbing, croquet, and even tug of war were all activities that were once contested.

But in several of the earliest Olympic Games, from 1912 until 1948, the Games' traditional list of sports was contested alongside a series of events in some very peculiar disciplines indeed— architecture, literature, music, painting, and sculpture!

When the ancient Greek Olympic Games were revived at the end of the 19th century, they were intended to be a worldwide celebration of both the body and the mind. The athletics events and other sporting events allowed athletes to show off their physical prowess, but alongside that more intellectual and creative competitions were organized to allow artists, writers, poets, and designers the chance to compete for Olympic medals as well.

The artistic Olympics were first introduced at the Stockholm Games in 1912, but they did not immediately prove popular and only 35 artists submitted work from around the world. Five winners were nonetheless chosen and awarded gold medals for their contributions. It was not until the 1928 Games in Amsterdam that the artistic Olympics truly took off. More than 1,000 works of art and literature were submitted to the competition, all of which were placed on display at a museum in the center of the Dutch capital. The event attracted so many entrants, in fact, that the original five categories had to be extended. Gold, silver, and bronze medals were awarded for specific achievements in fields such as town planning, painting, statues, lyric poetry, and orchestral music.

Although the artistic events continued to prove popular over the years that followed - with competitions like graphic printing, etching, and watercolor painting later added to the list - they were discontinued in the 1940s. Today they are not officially included as true Olympic events, and their prizes are not included in official Olympic medal hauls. Whether they will be resurrected in the future, and the artistic achievements of worldwide creators celebrated alongside sportsmen and women, however, remains to be seen!

GAYLORD PERRY AND
THE MEN ON THE MOON

Gaylord Perry is one of the most acclaimed Major League stars in baseball history. Born in North Carolina in 1922, he played for no less than eight different MLB teams throughout his career, becoming one of the game's most successful and reliable pitchers.

Like most pitchers, however, Perry's throwing ability was not matched by his hitting ability, and he was not well known for his skills as a batter. In fact, during the famous Space Race of the 1960s - when both Russian and American scientists were battling against one another to explore ever further into outer space - Perry once famously quipped in 1963 that, "They'll put a man on the moon before I hit a home run!"

As it happens, Perry went on to score just a single home run in his entire 20-year MLB career, when he struck a homer while playing for the San Francisco Giants on July 20, 1969 - just a few hours after the NASA spacecraft *Apollo 11* had landed astronaut Neil Armstrong on the surface of the Moon for the very first time. Perry's throwaway quip, it turned out, had been a perfectly accurate prediction!

HOW TO SHUFFLE A PACK OF CARDS

There are, of course, many different ways of shuffling a pack of cards. The cards can be thrown down and spliced between the hands, jumbling their order up that way. They can be riffled together, by being split between two piles and their corners run together. Or they can be messily swirled around a tabletop and then gathered back together, jumbling the cards together in one great sprawling mass. No matter how you do it, however, there is something truly extraordinary that is all but guaranteed about shuffling a deck of cards: no one in history will likely ever have produced the same shuffled order that you end up with.

It sounds too bizarre to be true, but the truth is that there are so many different possible combinations or "permutations" of a shuffled deck of 52 playing cards that whatever order you produce will likely never have been produced before. So just how many combinations are there?

Well, in mathematical terms, the precise number is equal to what is known as 52 factorial (or *52!* as it is written in mathematical terms). That calculation is equal to 52 multiplied by 51, multiplied by 50, multiplied by 49, multiplied by 48, and so on, right down to 1. Given that you are performing 52 multiplications there to get to the total number, needless to say, the answer to that calculation is staggeringly large: 80,658,175,170,943,878,571,660,636,856,403, 766,975,289,505,440,883,277,824,000,000,000,000!

So, there are 80.6 duovigintillion different combinations of cards in a shuffled deck. To put that number in perspective, that figure is larger than the number of atoms on the entire planet!

THE MIRACLE ON ICE

One of the most memorable events in sporting history took place at the 1980 Winter Olympic Games, which were held in Lake Placid, New York.

The "Miracle on Ice" was the name given to the semifinal of the men's Olympic ice hockey competition, which came down to a nail-biting game between the American team and the opposing Soviet Russian team, with each team attempting to secure a place in the ice hockey finals. Going into the semi, however, the odds were stacked massively in Russia's favor: the Soviet team had won all four of the previous Olympic gold ice hockey medals, beating the United States in all 12 of their last meets over the previous 20 years, from 1960 to 1980. In all that time, the Soviet Union had greatly outscored the American side, amassing a staggering total of 117 points to the USA's lowly 26. Just a week before the Olympics had even begun that year, the Soviets had defeated the US team 10-3 in a charity match at New York's Madison Square Garden. A fifth successive Soviet gold medal - and a fifth straight American defeat - seemed all but certain to happen.

As unlikely as it initially appeared, however, the young and relatively inexperienced American team (they had an average age of just 21) went on to outplay and outscore the Soviets. They fought back from 2-1 down at one stage to finish the game 4-2. It was an upset that would go down in Olympic history - as well as in American sporting history, with more than 36 million people tuning in to watch the game at home!

THE LONGEST TENNIS GAME IN HISTORY

Tennis surely has one of the most peculiar scoring systems of any major sport.

Games are scored using the numbers 15, 30, and 40, with players tying at 40–40 and then typically needing to score two consecutive points (first securing an "advantage" over their opponent, 40–A) in order to go on to win the game overall. A player then needs to win six games to take a set, with the best of five sets for the men, and three sets for the women, needed to take the match.

A quirk in the rules of some tennis competitions, however, is the so-called advantage set. Just as when a tennis game is tied 40–40 and a winning player has to win two consecutive points to secure victory, if a tennis set ends with the two players tied at six games each, 6–6, the players continue playing games until one of them wins two consecutive games outright, to ensure a two-game lead over their opponent. The final score of the set, therefore, could be 6–8.

Unfortunately, in this advantage set system, however, there is no limit to the number of games that can be played. So, if two players are similarly matched - and neither one can secure two consecutive victories and the necessary two-game lead over their opponent— then the entire match can potentially go on forever.

And that is almost what happened in 2010, in a Wimbledon tennis match between America's John Isner and France's Nicolas Mahut. With the match's scores deadlocked at 6–4, 3–6, 6–7, 7–6, and 6–6 in the final set, the two players were compelled to continue playing games until one of them won a two-game lead. As it happened, that took another 120 games, and a further two days of tennis. In total, the game went on to last for 11 hours and five minutes, with Isner eventually securing victory over Mahut in the final set, with a score of 70 games to 68!

HARRY CHITI:
THE MLB PLAYER WHO WAS
TRADED FOR HIMSELF

In April 1962, Major League catcher Harry Chiti was traded from the Cleveland Indians to the New York Mets, in exchange for a Mets player who was to be named and exchanged at a later date.

Born in Kincaid, Illinois, in 1932, at the time of the exchange Chiti already had several years' playing experience and had amassed an impressive track record as a glove-first catch with the Indians (and the Detroit Tigers, Baltimore Orioles, Kansas City A's, and Chicago Cubs before then). Despite being much in demand, however, at the Mets Chiti's impressive skills soon deserted him, it seems, and his performance on the New York diamond did not quite live up to expectations. Over the weeks that followed, Chiti played in 15 Mets games, batting just .195 (8–43).

Failing to make an impression on his newfound home team, Chiti played his final game with the Mets on June 10, after which the Mets decided to complete the deal and name the player they wanted to trade to the Cleveland Indians: Harry Chiti. When the Mets simply returned Chiti to the team they had early agreed to a deal with, he became the first and, to date, only player in Major League history to be traded for himself!

THE WORLD'S OLDEST CHESS SET

Chess is one of the world's oldest known board games. Variations of it have been played and enjoyed around the world for at least 1,500 years, with most chess historians and experts now believing the game likely developed from an ancient Indian board game called "chaturanga." From India, chaturanga was passed on to the neighboring Persian Empire, where it became known as "Shatranj." (It was at this point that the term "checkmate" was first introduced, as it comes from a Persian expression, *shah mat*, literally meaning "the king is dead"). From Persia, chess continued to spread westward into the Middle East and the Arab world, and from there into Europe sometime around the 6th century.

Perhaps what is now recognized as the world's oldest chess piece dates from around this time. In 2002, a small ivory playing piece - looking a little like a modern bishop from a game of chess but with a more rounded middle and a cross rather than a hat on its head - was discovered in the ruins of an ancient city in southern Albania. If it is indeed a chess piece, it likely dates back to the mid-400s CE. Chess pieces of a similar age have been uncovered across Eastern Europe, the Middle East, and Western Asia, with some of the earliest definitive chess pieces found in the Asian nation of Uzbekistan, dating back to CE 761.

One of the earliest known complete chess sets, however, is that of the so-called Lewis Chess Men, which were discovered on a remote Scottish island in 1831. A hoard containing more than 70 individual pieces, the Lewis chess set is thought to have been produced around 800 years ago! It is now partly on display in the famous British Museum in central London.

DID YOU KNOW?

○ There are 64 squares on a chessboard - half of which have playing pieces on them at the start of a game.

○ At the first Olympic Games, only gold and silver medals were handed out. The bronze medal was only added in 1904.

○ The German athlete Uwe Hohn is the only athlete ever to have thrown a javelin more than 100m in a competition, in 1984...

○ ...and it is likely he will be the only person ever to do so because competition javelins were made heavier two years after he did it!

○ A relay race baton is exactly 30 centimeters (11.911 inches) long.

○ An Olympic-sized swimming pool contains 2.5 million liters of water.

○ Olympic gold medals are only gold-plated. Inside they are actually silver!

LITERATURE   THE ARTS

THE SHIPWRECK THAT INSPIRED SHAKESPEARE

Have you heard of a play called *The Tempest*? It was perhaps William Shakespeare's last completed play, written sometime around 1610-1611 (about five years before his death). It tells the story of the crew of a ship who become stranded on a magical island during a wild ocean storm and fall under the spell of an exiled magician and duke known as Prospero.

The Tempest is one of Shakespeare's most loved and most performed plays, but few people realize that despite being filled with magical imps and sorcerers, the play is in fact based on a real-life event!

In 1609, around two years before *The Tempest* was completed and first performed in London, a ship called the *Sea Venture* set sail from England heading to the English colonies on the east coast of America. Midway through its Atlantic crossing, however, the *Sea Venture* sailed directly into an enormous hurricane, and the ship was smashed to pieces on the island of Bermuda.

When the ship failed to arrive in America, word was sent back to England that the ship and all those on-board most likely had been lost at sea. Just a few months after news of the loss became known back home, however, some of the crew members of the *Sea Venture* finally arrived at their destination. They had survived for a time on Bermuda, using the trees there to repair the *Sea Venture*. Against all odds, they had managed to complete their journey across the Atlantic.

When news of the *Sea Venture's* miraculous reappearance broke back in England, it understandably caused a sensation - and, if legend is to be believed, inspired the greatest playwright of the day to write his final play!

CHARLES DICKENS' LIFE ON STAGE

You likely know Charles Dickens best as an author, responsible for such popular and important stories as *A Tale of Two Cities*, *Oliver Twist*, and *A Christmas Carol*. But long before he started his career as a writer, Dickens himself had wanted to be an actor.

In fact, when he was still a teenager, Dickens was so fascinated and drawn to a life on the stage that he put himself forward to audition for a part in a new play that was set to be staged in Covent Garden in London. Dickens, who was just 19 years old at the time, learned the part and practiced for several days. However, on the morning of audition, he awoke with such a terrible cold that he missed his appointment. He never made it to the theatre to try out for the role and was so brutally disappointed by the entire affair that he abandoned his interest in pursuing a career as an actor. Instead, he went into writing, beginning first as a legal clerk and journalist, before finding the time to start writing his own stories and novels.

Although he abandoned his theatrical career before it had begun, Dickens' love of acting never left him. In fact, as his career as a writer began to take off, Dickens supplemented his writing work by giving live readings and performances of many of his books and stories - including a hugely popular one-man show in which he read and acted out *A Christmas Carol*!

THE AMERICANS OF
AMERICAN GOTHIC

American Gothic is one of the most famous paintings in the history of American art. Painted by the artist Grant Wood in 1930, the picture shows a stern-faced man and woman - the man holding a farmer's pitchfork - standing in front of white-fronted Gothic-style farmhouse.

When Wood first completed and displayed the painting back in the 1930s, it proved an instant hit with art fans and critics alike. Many began speculating as to who the couple in the painting were or were meant to represent. Even today, people presume that they are a middle-aged Midwestern married couple, likely appearing so unhappy and stern due to the effects of the Dust Bowl and the Great Depression that were ravaging America at the time. The actual truth of the painting, however, is rather less impressive!

Although Wood later stated that the painting was meant to represent the resilience of ordinary people, he was forced to come clean and admit that the couple in the painting are not an actual Midwestern couple. In fact, he modeled the figures on his own sister, Nan, and their family dentist, Byron McKeeby!

THE GAME THAT GAVE US FRANKENSTEIN

English author Mary Shelley's *Frankenstein* tells the terrifying tale of a deranged doctor who sews parts of dead bodies together to bring them back to life as a nightmarish monster. Incredibly, she wrote the story when she was just 19 years old! What is even more incredible, however, is the story behind the book itself.

In 1815, a volcano in Italy suddenly erupted, killing thousands of people in the surrounding area, and casting huge amounts of ash, dust, rock, and fumes into the air. As it spread throughout the atmosphere, the eruption disrupted almost the entire climate of mainland Europe. It blocked out the sunlight, lowered the temperatures, and triggered enormous thunderous storms and torrential downpours of rain. The effects of the disaster would be felt for the next three years.

Unfortunately for Mary Shelley, the eruption coincided with a trip around mainland Europe she was taking with her partner, the renowned poet Percy Bysshe Shelley, early in 1816. The volcano meant that instead of enjoying warm springtime days and a sunny summertime, much of Europe was wet, cold, and misty. Refusing to let the grim weather get them down, by the summertime, Mary and Percy had arrived in Switzerland. There they met up with one of Percy's friends - the fellow poet and writer, Lord Byron.

The views from Byron's home across the beautiful Lake Garda were magnificent - but unfortunately the weather in Switzerland was worse than ever before. The group were forced to shelter indoors for much of their time there. To pass the time, they began reading poems and stories, and frightening one another with the spookiest tales they could come up with. One night, Byron challenged the group to go and write a story that was scarier than any they had so far heard. Mary sat down with pen and paper, and that night wrote the outline for what would eventually become *Frankenstein*!

THE MAN WHO STOLE
THE *MONA LISA*

The *Mona Lisa* is perhaps the most famous painting in the world. But around a century ago, it was nowhere near as popular nor as well-known as it is today. What made this relatively small and surprisingly simple portrait of an unknown Venetian lady famous was something quite unexpected: it was stolen.

On the night of August 21, 1911, an Italian man named Vincenzo Perugia - who was working at the time in the famous Louvre art gallery where the painting was on display - remained behind after the gallery closed. He took the painting down off the wall and hid it under his coat. When the gallery reopened the following morning, Perugia simply walked out the front door carrying it with him.

When the painting's disappearance was noticed, the alarm was raised, and the theft quickly caused a sensation in the press all around the world. People everywhere were baffled as to how a painting could simply disappear, without anyone noticing it being taken. The police promptly investigated the theft, but with no leads to go on, the case rumbled on, unsolved, for many months.

In the meantime, Perugia had simply taken the painting home with him and hung it up on his wall. Finally, two years after he had stolen it, he broke cover and wrote to an art dealer in Florence, Italy, explaining that he would bring the painting to him in return for a cash reward. The deal went ahead, and in 1913 Perugia traveled to Rome - taking the *Mona Lisa* with him in the false bottom of his suitcase.

Of course, when the painting suddenly reappeared, the police had their lead and Perugia was arrested and briefly put in prison. In his defense, he later explained that he had (wrongly) believed

Napoleon had stolen the painting from Italy and wanted it to be put back on display in the country that had produced it. In the end, he got his wish: the *Mona Lisa* was for a short time exhibited in the famous Uffizi Gallery in Florence, before being returned to the Louvre.

THE MAN BEHIND
SHERLOCK HOLMES

The most famous detective in the world, Sherlock Holmes was created by the British author Sir Arthur Conan Doyle. Born in Edinburgh in 1859, Doyle originally trained as a doctor and wrote his first Sherlock Holmes stories during breaks between his patients at a medical practice in Plymouth. After the stories became popular, however, Doyle turned to writing full-time and before long had become one of the most successful and well-known authors in Victorian England.

Alongside his writing, however, Doyle had a somewhat unusual hobby for the time. He was fascinated by physical training and muscular development, and he eventually became interested in the newly emerging sport of bodybuilding. In 1901, he even helped to organize the world's first bodybuilding competition and acted as one of the three judges for the event, which was held at the famous Royal Albert Hall in London.

For a time, Doyle trained himself with one of the most famous musclemen of the time, a German weightlifter and athlete named Eugen Sandow. When he was later involved in a car accident in which his vehicle flipped upside down, pinning him to the ground by his neck, Doyle credited the physical strength training Sandow had taught him with his survival. Incredibly, Doyle walked away from the scene of the crash with little more than a few cuts and bruises!

VAN GOGH'S ONLY SALE

He might be one of the world's most popular and celebrated painters, but in his lifetime, Vincent Van Gogh only sold a single work of art. It was a colorful painting of a group of people picking grapes in an autumnal field, titled *The Red Vineyard near Arles*.

Van Gogh painted *The Red Vineyard* while staying near the city of Arles in the south of France in 1888. Considering it one of his best works, two years later he put it forward for exhibition at an exclusive art display, known as Les XX, in the city of Brussels, Belgium. By this time, Van Gogh had become somewhat well-known among his fellow painters but was not yet enjoying the same commercial success as some of his friends.

All that changed in 1890 when a Belgian art collector and fellow artist named Anna Boch agreed to purchase *The Red Vineyard* for the fairly impressive sum of 400 francs. Following the sale, Vincent excitedly wrote home to his brother to tell him that he had sold his first painting - though admitted that as Anna had been the sister of one of his friends, he felt guilty for charging her the gallery's price rather than offering her a discount!

Sadly, the painting was not only Van Gogh's first sale, but it was also his last. He grew ever more depressed and mentally troubled in the weeks that followed, and Van Gogh died later the same year at the age of just 37.

HOW *A CHRISTMAS CAROL* WAS A DICKENSIAN DISASTER

We have already found out that Charles Dickens enjoyed putting on performances of his books and stories to make up for his lost acting dream - but at least one of his most famous books proved such a costly mistake in his time that it nearly ended his career as a writer too!

Dickens wrote *A Christmas Carol* in the course of just a few weeks in the summer of 1843. In recent months, his book sales had begun to dwindle, and Dickens and his young family were in something of a financial black hole. Undeterred, he decided to press ahead with his writing and took the unusual step of taking complete creative control of the entire production of *A Christmas Carol*, by publishing it himself.

Dickens wanted the book to be read by as many people as possible, and so decided that its cover price should be kept as cheap as it could be. Unfortunately, he also wanted the book to be as lavish and as colorful as it could be, and so while the cover price was low, the cost of producing the leather-bound, golden-embossed, fully illustrated book was immensely high. As a result, despite the book selling out almost immediately, Dickens made little to any profit on it - and as it went into its second, and later third and fourth printings that year, his costs continued to skyrocket.

The financial situation went from bad to worse when several rival publishers began taking advantage of loopholes in England's copyright laws to produce their own cheaper versions of the story. When their editions began to prove just as popular as Dickens' own, his profits took another hit!

Happily, despite the financial disaster the book had turned into, Dickens managed to see out the year. He made enough money through the sales of tickets for readings he gave both at home in England and across the Atlantic in America. Within a matter of years, meanwhile, he had written his novel *David Copperfield*, which proved one of the biggest hits of his career and put him well on the road to fame and fortune.

DID YOU KNOW?

○ JK Rowling was paid just £2,500 for the first *Harry Potter* contract...

○ ...but the first book she wrote after the *Harry Potter* series was completed, was sold for £2 million!

○ The Spanish artist Pablo Picasso had a pet owl.

○ Charles Dickens once broke a woman's arm when he clumsily tried to dance with her.

○ The Oompa-Loompas in Roald Dahl's book *Charlie and the Chocolate Factory* were originally called "Whipple-Scrumpets."

○ In 2009, the thriller writer James Patterson signed the biggest book deal in publishing history, when he agreed to write 17 new books for his publisher, Hachette, in exchange for an estimated $150 million!

○ Dr. Seuss is credited with inventing the word "nerd."

MEDICINE

A PLAGUE OF DANCING

When you think of a "plague", you might think of the Black Death—the terrible so-called "bubonic" plague that swept across much of medieval Europe, killing millions of people as it went. What you are perhaps less likely to think of, however, is a plague of dancing.

It was in July 1518 that a woman known only as Frau Troffea, who lived in Strasbourg in eastern France, began unexpectedly and apparently for no reason to dance wildly and uncontrollably in the middle of the street. Before long, Troffea's bizarre performance had attracted a small crowd—and with an audience around her, Troffea continued dancing for days, and eventually, weeks.

As time went by, however, some people began joining Troffea in her dancing, and eventually there were dozens of people all wildly dancing in the streets of Strasbourg. But this was not quite the party-like dancing atmosphere you might expect it to be - because none of the dancers found that they could stop! Instead, they just danced and danced wildly, not stopping to eat, rest, or sleep. Some of them danced until they literally passed out through exertion, while some, it was reported at the time, danced for so long that they dropped down dead midway through their performance.

Precisely what caused this bizarre dancing mania - which swept like a plague through the people of the city - has been a medical mystery for hundreds of years. Some people have claimed that a bizarre form of poisoning might have caused the "dancing", and that the dancer's moves were actually fits and seizures. But in truth, the entire case remains unsolved - and is one of the most bizarre stories in the history of medicine!

CHANG AND ENG BUNKER: THE CONJOINED TWINS WHO CAPTIVATED THE WORLD

It's not a term that is much used today, but you might have heard of conjoined twins - a pair of siblings fused together at some part of their body - being referred to as "Siamese" twins.

The origin of that term is the country of Thailand, which was known as Siam until the late 1900s. And it was in Siam, in 1811, that one of the world's most famous pairs of conjoined twins were born.

Chang and Eng Bunker were born on May 11, 1811, in the Samut Songkhram area of what is now central Thailand. Joined together at the shoulder and chest from birth, the Bunker brothers were medical marvels, and their case soon attracted the attention of physicians from all around the world. In 1829, they relocated to the United States where they were observed by some of the world's foremost medical professionals - while at the same time exhibiting themselves at circuses and freak shows, earning an enormous amount of money in ticket sales.

After a decade in show business, the pair retired to North Carolina and went on to start families of their own after they married a pair of local sisters. They returned to touring and exhibitions later but largely remained out of the circus spotlight and lived relatively quiet lives. Choosing never to undergo the risky surgical procedure that would be needed to separate them, Chang and Eng remained joined together their entire lives. When Chang unexpectedly passed away at the age of 62 in 1874, Eng embraced his brother's body and died himself just a matter of hours later.

HOW THE ARTIFICIAL HEART CHANGED THE MEDICAL WORLD

Each time it beats, the heart pulses blood around our body's circulatory system, carrying the oxygen the rest of our body needs to function precisely to where it needs to be. At the same time, the heart pulls depleted blood back towards the lungs, where it can be replenished with more oxygen from the air we breathe. Then the process starts again.

This process is complex and vital, and the heart is one of the most important and delicate organs in the body. Yet what the above description means is that the human heart is in effect just a pump. It is similar to the kind of device that might be used to flush liquid out of a container or a flooded basement! And, for that reason, in the mid-1980s an inventor named Robert Jarvik was able to invent the world's first working artificial heart.

Known as the Jarvik-7, the first full artificial heart was implanted into a patient in 1982. The heart was constructed from two rubber hoses, which were connected to hoses and pumped rhythmically by an external electric current. Incredibly, even this early artificial heart proved a success, and the patient survived another 112 days after the operation to remove his own heart!

Since then, the technology Jarvik introduced has been improved and refined enormously. Modern artificial hearts are harmlessly and effectively implanted in patients all around the world every day.

THE WORLD'S FIRST BLOOD BANK

If a person who has had an accident or surgery loses a lot of blood, then it is important to replace that blood - using blood from a matching donor - as quickly as possible. This life-saving process has only been around 100 years. The first successful emergency blood donations were carried out on the battlefields and in the field hospitals of the Russian Front of World War I.

At that time, however, although wartime donors were happy to help out their injured comrades, fresh donated blood could only be kept and stored for a matter of days. If it was not used in that time, it had to be discarded for fear of making the patient who needed it unwell. In the mid-1930s, however, a Chicago-based physician named Bernard Fantus read about the efforts of Russian surgeons in storing and donating blood, and he started to perform his own experiments.

Eventually, Fantus developed a system that enabled him to remove blood from a donor, store it in refrigerated containers, and then safely pass it into a different patient several weeks later in what he called his "Blood Preservation Laboratory." Worried that that name might put people off from coming forward and donating their blood, however, Fantus later changed the name of his laboratory. In doing so, he established the world's first "Blood Bank" at the Cook County Hospital in Chicago in 1937.

AND THE WORLD'S FIRST VACCINE

Vaccines are truly remarkable feats of medical science, which have helped us all but eradicate several potentially deadly diseases from our world. But did you know that this extraordinary scientific development was first invented more than 200 years ago?

It was an English scientist named Edward Jenner who developed the very first successful vaccine way back in 1792. Several earlier attempts at vaccine-like injections and inoculations had been attempted. However, Jenner's - which relied on the findings of these early experiments - was the first that led to permanent resistance to disease.

The disease in question was a viral condition called smallpox, which at the time was a serious and potentially deadly illness. But Jenner knew of a far less serious condition called cowpox, which milkmaids often caught from their cows as they milked them. And he also knew that old English country folklore claimed that no one who had caught cowpox ever went on to develop smallpox.

To test this theory out, Jenner took some of the material from the hands of a local milkmaid who had developed cowpox and rubbed it onto the skin of a young boy, who Jenner knew had never had either disease. As he predicted, the boy fell slightly unwell with cowpox for a day or two but made a full recovery. Sometime later, Jenner repeated the same test, this time using viral material from a local case of smallpox. Incredibly, the folklore was proved right, and the boy remained entirely unharmed by smallpox.

Jenner's experiment was a breakthrough, and in the years that followed, it created a far greater understanding of how viral diseases are spread and can be treated. This in turn led to the development of the injected vaccines we still use to this day. In light of Jenner's experiments on the cowpox virus all those centuries ago, in fact, the word *vaccine* itself comes from "vacca," the Latin word for "cow"!

BABIES' BONES: HOW HUMAN SKELETONS ARE FORMED AFTER WE ARE BORN!

The average adult human being has 206 bones in their body.

Some of the smallest are inside our ears, while some of the largest are our lower ribs, our hips, and our thigh bones. Oddly, the arrangement of our bones is somewhat unbalanced: of those 206 bones, almost a third (64 in total) are in our arms and hands, while another 60 are found in our legs and feet. Odder still, however, is the fact that babies are born with more bones than adults!

When a baby is born, it actually has around 300 bones. As the child then grows up, some of these bones - including those of the skull - start to join together. That means a single bone in adulthood is made from several different bones joining together in childhood. Other bones start out as pieces of thick tissues called "cartilage" - the tough material from which your nose is made - that gradually become joined and covered by bone over time. This process continues for several years, throughout a person's teens, before eventually coming to an end by the time you are 25 years old, when all 206 bones are at long last in place.

But all of this leaves one question still unanswered: why do babies have more bones than adults at all? Well, it is all about flexibility! Because they have more bones than adults, babies' bodies are able to be compressed and bent more freely than adults' bodies - which is just as well, as it is this freedom of movement that allows babies to be born from inside their mothers!

THE PHILOSOPHER WHO LAUGHED HIMSELF TO DEATH

Whether it is the medicine that helps us when we are poorly when we are old, or the medical investigations that try to work out why someone has passed away, a large part of the medical world deals with what happens when our life comes to an end. But one of the strangest end-of-life stories in the medical world is that of an Ancient Greek philosopher named Chrysippus.

Chrysippus was born in Cilicia - a region of Ancient Greece now found in modern-day Turkey (**Türkiye**) - sometime around 279 BCE. An expert thinker in science, mathematics, and logic, he became known across the ancient world for his great intelligence and his extraordinary insight. Despite all his cleverness, however, Chrysippus still had a very ordinary sense of humor. In 206 BCE, at the age of 73, he happened to find something very funny indeed.

Chrysippus was out in his garden one day when he happened to find that his donkey had strayed from its field into his garden and eaten all of the figs that were growing there. Instead of getting angry, however, Chrysippus laughed it off, and joked to his housemaid that she should give the donkey some wine with which to wash the figs down. Simply following her master's orders, the housemaid did just as she had been asked and gave the donkey some wine to drink, making it drunk. The old philosopher apparently found this sight so hilariously funny that he collapsed in a fit of uncontrollable laughter and died instantly, having laughed himself to death!

JULIUS CAESAR AND THE CAESAREAN SECTION

You might have heard of an operation called a caesarean section, or C-section. It is a procedure, often performed in an emergency, in which a baby is removed from its mother by surgery rather than through a natural childbirth down the mother's birth canal.

If you've heard of that procedure before, however, you might also have heard the story that this procedure is named after the Roman emperor Julius Caesar, who was apparently born this way in 100 BCE.

Unfortunately, that bit of this story is apparently completely untrue. The doctors of Ancient Rome did have an equivalent procedure to the caesarean section, but they did not name it after one of their most famous emperors. That is because the only way in which they knew to carry this procedure out *always* resulted in the mother dying during childbirth. As we know that Julius Caesar's mother lived long into her old age, he cannot have been born this way.

Instead, the word *caesarean* has nothing to do with the name Caesar at all, but instead comes from a Latin word meaning simply "to cut." Its similarity to Julius Caesar's name - and the myth that this operation is named in his honor - is ultimately just a coincidence!

DID YOU KNOW?

- The human brain is three times larger than most other animals our size.

- The strongest bone in the body is the thigh bone...

- ...while the strongest substance in the human body is the enamel that coats our teeth!

- Between 60%–70% of the human body is water.

- Your nose can detect 10,000 different smells.

- The human brain cannot feel pain.

- Your armpit is properly called your "axilla"...

- ...while your big toe is called the "hallux"!

EXPLORATION

CAPTAIN COOK'S LAST VOYAGE

Captain James Cook is one of the world's most famous and furthest traveled explorers. Born in England in 1728, he joined the British Royal Navy while still a boy. Cook gradually worked his way up through the ranks until he came to the attention of the Admiralty - the part of the government in England responsible for overseeing naval operations. Working with a scientific organization in England known as the Royal Society, in the mid-1700s, the Admiralty became interested in furthering Britain's interests around the world. It was actively looking for an experienced navigator, map-reader, and captain to oversee explorations to the other side of the world. Cook was chosen to lead the first of what would go on to be three amazingly long voyages from England to the Pacific Ocean, on board his flagship, the HMS *Endeavour*.

Cook's voyages were extraordinary as much of that part of the world was uncharted at the time, and the Admiralty had no idea what or who he was going to encounter on his journeys. Nevertheless, he set sail undaunted and over the next two decades successfully explored much of southeast Asia, Australia, New Zealand, and the islands of the Pacific.

For all of his work, you might expect Cook's life to end with him being richly rewarded for his exploits back home in England - but on the third of his voyages to the Pacific Ocean in 1779, Cook was killed in a dispute while visiting the Hawaiian Islands. The precise circumstances around his death have remained somewhat mysterious ever since. Some people claim the islands' natives attacked him and his crew in an attempt to rob them, while others now believe that he was killed in defense after he and his men tried to kidnap the islands' chief. Whatever the truth, one of the greatest explorers that England - and indeed the world - has ever seen died far away from home, having never completed his final journey.

"THE WORST JOURNEY IN THE WORLD"

If you had to imagine what the worst journey in the world was, you might pick one that occurred in the cold, the wind, the snow, and the dark. And according to a British explorer named Apsley Cherry-Garrard, you'd be quite right!

In 1910, Cherry-Garrard joined the crew of a scientific polar research ship called the *Terra Nova* that was headed to Antarctica. Its captain was the renowned polar explorer, Sir Robert Falcon Scott. The ship's crew had two goals in mind for their trip to the Antarctic: first, they wanted to collect emperor penguin eggs, so that scientists back in England could examine them, and second, Scott wanted to lead some of his men to the South Pole, becoming the first people in history to trek there.

Cherry-Garrard was initially intended only to participate in the first part of this exploration. Having arrived in Antarctica, he joined up with the ship's second-in-command, Edward Wilson, in trekking across the snowfields to the emperor penguins' breeding grounds. Unfortunately, the birds nest during the Antarctic winter. So, although the explorers were crossing the continent in July, they were doing so in complete darkness, and in temperatures that frequently fell as low as −77.5° F. Cherry-Garrard later wrote about this journey in a book he published on his return to England several years later, which he called *The Worst Journey in the World!*

A TRIP TO THE SOUTH POLE

But what about Captain Scott? Tragically, his attempt to trek his party of men from the Terra Nova to the South Pole was less successful.

Scott and 11 other men set off for the pole on October 24, traveling with a team of ponies, sled dogs, and several motorized sledges. Unfortunately, the sledge motors quickly broke down in the bitter conditions, the ponies were killed, and the dog team and their handlers had to be sent back to the ship. Just five men went on to complete the journey, arriving at the pole on January 17, 1912 - only to discover that a rival explorer, the Norwegian Roald Amundsen, had beaten them to it by around five weeks!

On their return to the coast, however, Scott and his remaining men faced the worst weather of the entire journey. One man dropped down dead while walking across the ice field. When they pitched their tent in an attempt to see out a devastating storm, another of the men, Captain Oates, sacrificed himself, He wandered off into the Antarctic wastes, hoping that his disappearance would help the others ration their dwindling supplies. In the end, however, Captain Oates' valiant sacrifice was unneeded, as all the remaining men perished in their tent as the worst of the polar weather closed in.

When news of his death broke back home in England, Robert Scott was declared a hero and has remained a much-admired figure in the history of exploration ever since.

SHACKLETON'S LOST SHIP

Another polar explorer whose trips to the coldest parts of the world ended in disaster was Ernest Shackleton. Born in Ireland in 1874, Shackleton studied in England and joined the Royal Navy in in the late 1800s.

In the early 1900s, Shackleton enlisted in the crew of one of Captain Scott's earlier journeys to Antarctica, returning home in 1913 with a taste for polar exploration. He led his own expedition there the following year, planning to walk across Antarctica - via the South Pole - and sail home from the opposite side of the continent. Like Scott before him, however, Shackleton's expedition did not quite go to plan.

When he and his men arrived off the coast of Antarctica in 1914, their ship, the *Endurance*, quickly became stuck amid a sea of floating blocks of ice. As the sea continued to freeze around them, the ship became completely trapped. As the wintery conditions continued, the ice became thicker and thicker and eventually crushed the ship. Now stranded on the ice floes of the Antarctic Ocean, Shackleton and his men floated aimlessly with no sense of where they were for the next ten months.

In 1915, however, incredibly, the crew of the *Endurance* sighted land and managed to paddle their way towards an island in the South Shetland Islands, now known as Elephant Island. Leaving the majority of his men on the island - - here they lived off a diet of seal meat and seabird eggs - Shackleton and a handful of his remaining crew set off again in the hopes of arranging a rescue mission. They arrived at the larger island of South Georgia, having navigated 800 miles of dangerous ocean, and amazingly from there managed to launch a rescue mission to retrieve the rest of their crew four months later.

Incredibly, despite this year-long ordeal, not one of Shackleton's crew died.

THE MAN WHO VANISHED IN THE AUSTRALIAN BUSH

In 1802, a British man named William Buckley was found guilty of theft in a court in England. At the time, English courts were able to punish thieves not simply by sending them to jail, but by sending them to the other side of the world! Buckley was sentenced to "transportation" and was promptly sent to work as a laborer in England's growing colonies in Australia.

Having arrived at Port Philip Bay in Australia, however, Buckley escaped from the labor town where he was employed in 1803 and vanished. The Australian Bush was known to be so inhospitable, however - thanks to the soaring temperatures, lack of water, and numerous venomous snakes and insects - that Buckley was presumed by those in charge in Port Philip to have died. In truth, however, he survived in the most remarkable way possible.

Having fled from his work at Port Philip Bay, Buckley happened to bump into a local tribe of indigenous Australians, known as the Wallarranga tribe of the Wathaurong nation. The tribe accepted Buckley as one of their own, offering him food, water, and shelter, and Buckley went on to live with his newfound community for the next 32 years.

In 1835, Buckley heard news through the indigenous community that another English ship had been spotted off the coast of Australia, and that some of the local native people were planning to attack it and kill the crew. Instead, Buckley intercepted the attack and revealed himself to the arriving Englishmen, who were astonished to hear his story. He went on to work as an interpreter and mediator before moving to Van Diemen's Land (Tasmania).

GUDRID THORBJARNARDÓTTIR: THE FIRST FEMALE EXPLORER OF THE NEW WORLD

When it comes to early American explorers, you might think of figures like Henry Hudson and Christopher Columbus. One name that deserves to be thought of in much the same way, however, is that of Gudrid Thorbjarnardóttir.

Also known as *Gudrid Víðförla* , or "Gudrid the Well-Travelled," Thorbjarnardóttir was an Icelandic explorer born in the 11th century, and one of the most famous and furthest-traveled female explorers in history. Alongside her husband, Thorfinn Karlsefni, she embarked on several early explorations of the Arctic and eastern regions of North America, following in the footsteps of the early Viking explorer Leif Eriksson. Together, they established a new community in North America.

It was there, sometime in the early 1000s, that Gudrid gave birth to the couple's son, Snorri. He became the first westerner ever born in the western hemisphere, while Gudrid went down in history as the first woman to give birth in what eventually became known as the "New World."

THE EXPLORER WHO GAVE HIS NAME TO AMERICA

Born in Florence in 1454, Amerigo Vespucci initially worked as a banker under the famous Medici family before joining a Spanish exploratory journey to the New World in 1499. Serving as the ship's mapmaker and astronomer, Vespucci set sail alongside the Spanish explorer Alonso de Ojeda and arrived in South America several months later. Sailing down the coast, Vespucci's expedition likely reached the Amazon River, before heading north once again to Trinidad, the Gulf of Mexico, and Haiti. Wrongly believing that they had arrived in Asia, the expedition set off back home to Europe to report their discovery.

In 1501, a second expedition was launched, this time with Vespucci taking an even more important role in the crew. Arriving once again on the coast of Brazil, Vespucci this time headed south - perhaps reaching as far south as Argentina - before returning to Lisbon the following year. Having completed this journey, however, Vespucci became convinced that the lands he and his men were finding on the opposite side of the ocean were not Asia, but an entirely New World.

As news of his discoveries spread, an account of Vespucci's travels was published in 1507 in which it was suggested this new world be named "ab Americo, Inventore...quasi Americi terram sive Americam" - meaning "from Amerigo the Discoverer...as if it were the Land of Americus." The name soon stuck, and the New World has been known as "America" ever since!

THE DARIEN SCHEME: SCOTLAND'S FAILED ATTEMPT AT A NEW WORLD COLONY

During the Age of Exploration, many European nations set off around the world establishing trade posts and colonies all over the globe. Some were more successful than others: France, England, Spain, Portugal, and the Netherlands all went on to build immensely powerful empires that sprawled over all the world's continents. England's northern neighbor Scotland, however, was less successful.

In 1693, a Scottish explorer and trader named William Paterson put forward a plan. He suggested that Scotland should establish a trading post in Central America, in modern-day Panama, so that it could start to control trade between the Atlantic and Pacific Oceans. The scheme was ambitious but popular, and more than half a million pounds was quickly invested in Paterson's project, funding the five ships he believed would be needed to carry it out. The vessels set sail from Leith Harbor, on the coast of the city of Edinburgh, in 1698 headed to Panama. Their arrival on the other side of the Atlantic, however, was to prove a disaster.

First of all, the settlers - many of whom were already sick from the journey over - arrived in a swampy wasteland, known as Darien, that they found to be filled with biting bugs, mosquitos, caiman, and snakes. None of the surrounding land was farmable, and none of the water they could find was drinkable. Before long, some of the settlers began succumbing to their ailments and starvation, forcing others to move inland looking for better and more profitable land. What they found instead were tribes of natives, with whom they tried to barter their belongings in exchange for food, water, and medicine. Unfortunately, the confused natives had little use for the clothing, wigs, and Scottish whisky the Darien explorers had brought with them, and their potential trades failed.

Eventually, the entire project was abandoned, and the survivors of the failed Darien scheme returned home soon afterward. Scotland never again attempted to establish an independent colony of its own, and instead joined with England to create the United Kingdom in 1707.

DID YOU KNOW?

○ Christopher Columbus was Italian - but his journey to America was funded by Spain!

○ Ferdinand Magellan named the Pacific Ocean...

○ ...while when he arrived there, Captain Cook named the islands we now know as Tonga the "Friendly Islands."

○ Human beings have explored more of the Moon than we have the depths of the ocean.

○ The deepest part of the ocean - the Mariana Trench - was not explored until 1960.

○ Marco Polo was born in Venice - so the airport in Venice, Italy, is now called Venice Marco Polo, or VCE!

○ The most remote point on the surface of the Earth is in the middle of the Pacific Ocean. It is called "Point Nemo."

DISASTERS

THE LONDON TORNADO OF 1091

It is an odd fact that Europe gets more tornadoes than the United States—and one of the countries with the most tornadoes per square mile of territory in the entire world is not the USA, but the UK.

Of course, most of the twisters that touch down in the UK are nowhere near as powerful as those that strike the so-called "Tornado Alley" of the American Midwest. But almost a thousand years ago, a powerful whirlwind equivalent in strength to those we might find in the US today did indeed touch down in central London, devastating the medieval city.

It was on October 17, 1091, that an equivalent F4 tornado appeared to form above London. As it moved through the city, it destroyed the original wooden London Bridge, as well as 600 homes, and several major churches. Among them was the famous St. Mary-Le-Bow Church in the center of the city; incredibly, four huge 26-foot rafters from the church's roof were picked up by the twister and thrown down into the earth so forcefully that only four feet of wood remained visible above the ground!

The storm may have been strong, but amazingly there were only two reported fatalities -not bad given that the densely packed city was at the time home to over 18,000 people!

THE GREAT MOLASSES FLOOD

One of the strangest and most devastating disasters in modern history took place in Boston, Massachusetts, in 1919 when a huge storage tank full of molasses burst open, spilling over two million gallons of syrup into the city's streets. Weighing over 12,000 tons, the wave of molasses swept down through Boston like a tsunami, moving at an estimated 35 mph and destroying almost everything and everyone it washed over. In the disaster, 150 people were injured, while a further 21 people—as well as a great many horses (approximately 12) lost their lives.

Quite what caused the tank to burst has been the subject of debate ever since. The most likely explanation, however, is that the weather was to blame.

Although the disaster took place in January, the day on which it happened - January 15 - had been noticeably warmer than the preceding week. This sudden upward shift in temperature likely caused the previously freezing cold molasses to expand, rupturing the tank and causing its outer metal casing to buckle. Once that had happened, there was no stopping the resulting liquid from spilling out.

THE TUNGUSKA EVENT

Another bizarre disaster from the early 1900s took place in Siberia - the freezing wastes of northern Russia - in 1908.

Early on the morning of June 30, a farmer in Siberia reported seeing "the sky split in two" and fire rain down all around the surrounding forests. There was then a sudden explosion, like "cannons firing" in the distance, and a shockwave that knocked a man from his feet and threw him several yards across the ground. In the aftermath of the explosion, researchers in the area found that hundreds and hundreds of trees and buildings had been completely flattened over an area of more than 800 square miles.

But what was the cause of the mysterious and devastating Siberian explosion, that has long since become known as the "Tunguska Event"? Scientists now believe that a gigantic asteroid or comet must have flown into the Earth's atmosphere above Siberia. It either exploded in the sky - throwing out a vast wave of power like an explosion through the air - or else struck the Earth, causing an earthquake-like tremor. The strike at Tunguska in Siberia, ultimately, is one of the most powerful asteroid strikes ever recorded.

THE ERUPTION OF KRAKATOA

Krakatoa is the name of a gigantic volcano that lies in a chain of islands between Java and Sumatra, two of the westernmost islands in Indonesia. In August 1883, the volcano erupted, generating the largest and most powerful volcanic activity that has ever been recorded.

Volcanic activity in the area had been building for several months previously, with earthquakes and underground tremors being felt as far away as Australia. Plumes of ash began to spill from the volcano in June, but the eruption itself did not begin until the end of August. Early on the morning of August 27, a series of four immense explosions tore through the area.

The first of these enormous blasts was strong enough to trigger a tsunami that swept through the surrounding seas. The third of the four, however, was the most powerful of all. It exploded with the same amount of power as 10,000 nuclear bombs. The explosion was loud enough to be heard thousands of miles away in Mauritius, in the middle of the Indian Ocean, and even in Perth, on the west coast of Australia. Incredibly, this one sound alone is now credited with being the loudest sound in human history.

THE YEAR WITHOUT A SUMMER

Another Indonesian volcano, Mount Tambora, erupted with similar violence in 1815. This time, the eruption threw more than ten cubic miles of ash and rocky material into the sky, which continued to drift high into the Earth's atmosphere. Incredibly, the Tambora eruption in 1815 produced so much material that in its aftermath, the entire climate of the world was affected.

The effects of the Tambora eruption were felt nowhere more so than in Europe, where the following year, 1816, became known as "The Year Without A Summer." As the material in the atmosphere continued to disrupt weather and climate systems around the world, temperatures in Europe dropped dramatically. The summer of 1816 was the coldest recorded in any year of the last millennium.

The unpleasant weather caused crops to fail and triggered floods and frosts that ruined food supplies for the next 12 months. Elsewhere around the world, the rainy seasons in Africa and Asia were affected by the Tambora eruption too, while in America, the material from the volcano caused a persistent hazy red fog that lingered in the sky for the entire year.

THE LAKE NYOS DISASTER

Perhaps one of the strangest and most tragic disasters in recent decades took place in Western Africa in 1986.

It was on August 26 that year that a gigantic cloud of natural carbon dioxide gas bubbled up from the bed of Lake Byos, a large volcanic lake in the West African country of Cameroon. There was no warning that the disaster was about to occur, but the locals who lived around the lake and who survived what happened later reported hearing a distant rumbling sound, rather like a far-off thunderstorm, and smelling a peculiarly unpleasant aroma the air. Shortly afterward, however, the cloud of gas burst forth out of the lake - and as the toxic gas swept outwards around the lake, it killed almost everyone who breathed it in.

Incredibly, some 1,700 people were killed by the disaster, as well as thousands more cattle, and many hundreds of thousands more wild animals, birds, fish, and insects. The cause of the disaster was not immediately clear, but when an investigation was launched, it became clear. Some kind of event - perhaps a landslide or earthquake - had triggered the release of the gas from below the ground, causing it to bubble up through the lake.

THE PEPSI JUICE FLOOD

Boston is not the only city to have experienced a flood of something other than water - as recently as 2017, the Russian town of Lebedyan suffered a similar fate. On April 25, the roof of a PepsiCo warehouse in the town suddenly and unexpectedly collapsed.

The Lebedyan warehouse was the regional center for all the Pepsi company's operations in the area. As such, it contained several immense vats of fruit juices and other liquids. The falling masonry from the warehouse's roof quickly overturned and ruptured the vats, and as a result, over seven million gallons of juice were sent spilling out into the surrounding town.

The disaster left enormous puddles of brown soda and fruit syrup dotted all over the area, and there were concerns that the juices involved in the flood might ruin the local water supply and contaminate the nearby river. Thankfully, not only was the local waterway largely unaffected by the disaster, but there were also just two reported injuries - both factory workers, hurt by the falling roof - and no fatalities!

THE DAY IT RAINED GOLF BALLS

For centuries, people around the world have reported bizarre raining events, with everything from huge schools of fish to hundreds of live frogs said to have fallen from the skies at various times and locations. Often, these freak "weather" events are said to have been caused by tornadoes and similar storms. These have the incredible ability to lift things up into the air and often transport them - sometimes undamaged - a great many miles before depositing them back on the ground. If such a storm passes over rivers or lakes, huge numbers of live animals can be picked up by the tornado, neatly explaining how these freak downpours often involve marine and aquatic animals.

One of the strangest of these occurrences, however, happened in Punta Gorda, Florida, in 1969. According to reports from the time, the surrounding town was suddenly deluged with huge numbers of golf balls that fell from the sky! Just like with the fish and the frogs, however, it seemed the bizarre disaster was the work of a tornado. The storm had apparently broken out over a nearby golf course and driving range. It had simply picked up all the loose balls lying on the greens and fairways (and, no doubt, at the bottom of the lake!).

DID YOU KNOW?

○ Although the explosion of Krakatoa was incredibly violent, it was the shockwaves and tsunamis it caused that killed the most people. Over 300 villages were destroyed by the rising seas that the eruption caused.

○ Despite destroying most of the city, the famous Great Fire of London in 1666 caused just six fatalities.

○ The eruption of Mount Vesuvius that famously flattened the village of Pompeii in CE 79 also flattened another town - the nearby resort of Herculaneum.

○ In 1995, a volcano on the Caribbean island of Montserrat began to erupt and has continued to erupt ever since. Two-thirds of the island's population has had to be evacuated and has never returned.

○ The biggest earthquake ever recorded struck Chile in 1960. It measured 9.5 on the Richter scale.

○ The winds in a tornado can spin at over 250 mph.

○ 2005's Hurricane Katrina caused nearly $150 billion in damage.

GENERAL KNOWLEDGE

THE CHILD WHO GAVE US A "GOOGOL"

In English, we're used to names of big numbers - like million, billion, and trillion - all sounding the same. But in 1920, while writing his book *Mathematics and the Imagination*, the American mathematician Edward Kasner gave us a new word for an extraordinarily big number: a googol.

Kasner was writing about the mathematical properties of immense numbers, when he needed a name for a figure equivalent to a number one followed by 100 zeroes. In mathematical terms, just such a number would properly be known as ten duotrigintillion - but Kasner wanted something snappier for his book. So, he turned to his nine-year-old nephew Milton to make up a word on the spot. The word Milton came up with was *googol*.

One followed by 100 zeroes has been known as a "googol" ever since - but Milton's random invention does not end there. A one followed by a googol of zeroes is known as a googolplex, while a googolplexian is the number ten raised to the power of a googolplex - or in arithmetical terms, $10^{(10^{(10^{100})})}$!

WHY SANDWICHES ARE CALLED...SANDWICHES!

While it was a nine-year-old boy that gave us the googol, elsewhere in our language it is not uncommon to find words named after, rather than by, people.

The diesel engine, for instance, is named after an inventor called Rudolph Diesel. Pilates exercises are named after Joseph Pilates, who devised them. And even the cowboy's famous Stetson hat is named after a Philadelphia hatmaker named John B. Stetson. Surely one of the most peculiar words named after a real person, however, is the sandwich.

Sandwiches are named after an 18th-century English nobleman named John Montagu, who held the title of Earl of Sandwich. According to tradition, the Earl of Sandwich is said to have been a keen gambler and did not like to stop his card games and betting rounds in order to sit down to meals. Instead, he asked to be served slices of cold meat and bread at the card table itself - and as he ate one with the other, he inadvertently invented the sandwich!

THE MAN WHO BOUGHT ALASKA

Alaska has been a US state since it was admitted into the Union in January 1959; it was America's 49th state overall, with Hawaii joining just seven months later. Before then, however, Alaska had been American territory for almost a century - when, in one of the most curious events in American history, it was literally bought from Russia for $7.2 million.

The so-called Alaska Purchase took place in 1867. Previously, the area we now know as Alaska had been owned and controlled by Russia. However, with Russia having recently faced a costly defeat in the Crimean War, the Russian ruler, Alexander II, began looking at new ways to inject money into his economy. Although Russia controlled Alaska, few Russian people had chosen to settle there, so Alexander put the entire territory up for cash sale.

The deal caught the attention of the US Secretary of State, William Seward. He saw Alaska as a way of expanding America's territory northward and westward. It could also potentially open new avenues of trade with Canada and Asia. Negotiations soon got underway, and a price of $7.2 million - equivalent to just 36 cents per acre - was eventually agreed. Not everyone was quite so keen to see half a million square miles of wilderness added onto America in exchange for millions of dollars of cash, however, and opponents to Seward's scheme dismissed the purchase as "Seward's Ice Box!"

Nonetheless, the sale went ahead, and Alaska came to be controlled by the US Department of State. Over time, moves to upgrade its status in the USA grew, until finally, it achieved statehood almost a century after Seward's Alaska Purchase had been made.

THE BEAR THAT LIVED AT THE TOWER OF LONDON

The Tower of London is one of England's most famous and most popular landmarks. Work on the medieval tower began way back in 1078 and continued expanding over the next 300 years. It was completed in the late 14th century. Today it is little more than a tourist attraction and museum, where the British royal family's Crown Jewels are kept on display. However, over the years, the Tower has been used as a prison, a public record office, an armory, the Royal Mint (where new coins are produced) - and, perhaps strangest of all, a zoo!

It was the medieval King John who first began keeping animals at the Tower of London during his reign in the late 1100s and early 1200s. His successors continued to build the royal menagerie over the centuries to come, adding the likes of a rhino, a hyena, a leopard, several wolves, and lynxes, and even - during the reign of Henry III - a polar bear, to the royal collection.

The bear King Henry III kept at the Tower of London was originally a gift from the Norwegian King Haakon IV. According to reports, the bear seemed to be perfectly happy with its new home - not least given that it was taken from its enclosure at the Tower every morning and walked down to the River Thames to swim and hunt for fish!

THE DOG THAT ATE
STEINBECK'S MASTERPIECE

It's one of the oldest school excuses going: "The dog ate my homework!" But in 1936, a dog really *did* eat someone's homework - and that someone was one of the most famous authors of the 20th century!

A "minor tragedy" is how the future Pulitzer prize-winning author John Steinbeck referred to what happened on May 27, 1936, when his beloved pet dog, a setter named Toby, ate much of the first handwritten draft of his future bestseller *Of Mice and Men*. Around half of the manuscript was destroyed in the incident, which Steinbeck later wrote told his editor was roughly equivalent to two months' work.

Happily, though understandably disappointed with having to begin the book again, Steinbeck saw the funny side of the event and did not seem too angry with Toby. "I was pretty mad," he wrote, but added that, "I'm not sure Toby didn't know what he was doing when he ate the first draft...the poor little fellow may have been acting critically."

Just as well Toby did not eat the entire book, then. Published in 1937, *Of Mice and Men* has since gone on to be recognized as one of the greatest books in modern American literature!

THE WORLD'S FIRST SKYSCRAPER

If you were to picture a skyscraper in your mind, you might imagine an enormous glassy building towering far off into the sky, dozens of floors above you. But the world's very first skyscraper was nothing of the sort!

The Home Life Insurance Building was built in Chicago, Illinois, in 1885. In comparison to modern skyscrapers, however, it stood just ten stories high, at a total height of 138 feet. That was still extremely tall for the time, however, and the building's planning and construction took several years to get right. Before its completion, many of even the world's most famous and experienced architects were not convinced that a simple metal skeleton of girders could hold up such a large building!

After the Home Life Insurance Building was finished, however, the engineering and technology behind it soon improved. Before long, it had been overtaken by several larger, taller, and grander buildings. Within a matter of decades, in fact, the Home Life building was seen as so outdated that it was decided to pull it down. The building was demolished in 1931 - exactly the same year the Empire State Building, which is ten times its height, was completed in New York!

TOY STORY 2: THE MOVIE THAT WAS ALMOST LOST

Since the late 1990s, animated movies have shifted away from the hand-drawn films of the past and into the new computer-generated movies of the present. Today, dozens of animated movies are released every year that are entirely created digitally, with images developed and coded on screens and in complex computer programs. In the early days of these technologies, however, it often took several years to complete a single movie. That's at least one of the reasons why *Toy Story 2*, the follow-up to the first entirely computer-animated feature film, 1995's *Toy Story*, took four years to complete.

One other reason why the film was delayed, however, was that it was almost deleted from the Pixar computer system altogether!

One day during the movie's production, while the animators were working on a single scene part way through the film, an error in the film's computer code led to the program automatically and unstoppably deleting line after line of the surrounding code, threatening to wipe out the entire film. Unable to stop the computer from running the code, the animators could only watch as Woody's hat suddenly vanished, followed unstoppably by everything else. Without any other available fix, the computer was unplugged, and the servers shut down - but it was too late. By the time the error had been stopped, some 90% of the movie had been deleted.

As luck would have it, however, one of the animation team, Galyn Susman, was on maternity leave and had a copy of the movie at home, from which a backup could later be salvaged. Without that stroke of good luck, however, the entire movie could have been lost for good!

DANIEL BAKEMAN:
THE LAST SURVIVOR OF
THE REVOLUTIONARY WAR

The American Revolutionary War was fought from 1775 to 1783. Incredibly, however, the last surviving veteran of the conflict died in 1869, almost a century after the war came to an end.

He may not be the most famous or most celebrated of American military figures, but Daniel Frederick Bakeman was the last surviving Revolutionary soldier. Born on October 9, 1759, in New York - which was still, at the time, part of British America Bakeman served as a private for the last four years of the war while he was just a teenager. He even took part in the famous Battle of Johnstown in 1781.

When the war was over, Bakeman married and started a family, eventually settling in Arcade, New York, and later the nearby town of Freedom. He was last recorded as living in Freedom in the 1860 US census - at the age of 100 - alongside his wife, one of his daughters, Susan, and one of his many grandchildren, Jacob. Incredibly, he went on to live for another nine years after that, and died on April 5, 1869, at the age of 109. A bronze plaque on his grave today commemorates him as the "Last Pensioner of the War For Independence."

DID YOU KNOW?

○ Dogs are mentioned 18 times in the Bible...

○ ...but cats aren't mentioned once!

○ The letter Z used to the up the front part of the alphabet before the Romans got rid of it and the letter G took its place!

○ Two is the only even prime number.

○ Venus is the hottest planet in our solar system, despite being further from the Sun than Mercury.

○ The Romans used to play soccer using an inflated pig's bladder as a ball.

○ The most commonly struck key on a computer keyboard isn't a letter - it's the space bar!

CONCLUSION

And with that final super interesting story, your book of super interesting stories is complete!

We sincerely hope you have enjoyed the past 100 or so journeys through the stranger and more fascinating parts of the world, its history, and our knowledge of everything in it—from polar explorers to wartime heroes, medical breakthroughs, peculiar tragedies, strange disappearances, and bizarre animals. Along the way, we've met a deranged king, a long-lived soldier, an innovative Hollywood starlet, a mathematical genius, and more than a few incredible thinkers, inventors, and minds.

Here too, remember, was the tale of the archduke who escaped one attempt on his life...only to fall foul of another! Plus, the tale of the exploding cigar, the finches that inspired Charles Darwin, the author who predicted the moons of Mars, and the explorer who truly risked it all in the depths of Antarctica - only to be pipped at the final post!

So which tale was your favorite? Which fact or factoid sticks out most in your mind? Why not take a peek back through these pages now to remind yourself of just how bizarre, how surprising, and how super interesting the world can be!

Printed in Dunstable, United Kingdom